# The World Economic Crisis

*a Commonwealth Perspective*

Commonwealth Secretariat, Marlborough House, London SW1

Published by
The Commonwealth Secretariat

May be purchased from
Commonwealth Secretariat Publications
Marlborough House
London SW1Y 5HX

ISBN 0 85092 183 X

Price £1.00

# Foreword by Commonwealth Secretary-General

Commonwealth Heads of Government, meeting in Lusaka in August 1979, expressed their grave concern with the deterioration in the world economic situation and prospects. In their search for remedies, they requested me to commission a Group of Experts 'to investigate and report on the factors inhibiting structural change and a sustained improvement in economic growth' and to 'identify specific measures by which developed and developing countries, Commonwealth and non-Commonwealth, might act to reduce or eliminate such constraints as a matter of urgency'. The Report of the Group of Experts is contained within these covers.

Since the Lusaka meeting, the global economic crisis has deepened and there is now considerable pessimism about the ability of nations to control world economic trends. The Group of Experts, consisting of distinguished persons from both North and South, has highlighted the grave consequences of the present situation for the peoples of the world, particularly those in the developing countries. The Report, which does not aim to cover the field but to focus on some acutely critical areas, shows that it is within the capacity of the world community, acting collectively and in harmony, to respond effectively to the crisis and to overcome current constraints on structural change in the world economy and on sustained economic growth. In the selected areas of its inquiry, the Experts' Group puts forward a number of specific practical measures directed towards achieving a more equitable, prosperous and stable world society.

The Experts themselves were drawn from a representative range of developed and developing countries: Australia, Canada, India, Malaysia, New Zealand, Nigeria, Sri Lanka, Trinidad and Tobago, the United Kingdom and Zambia. It must be emphasised, however, that they have prepared and signed the Report in their personal capacities and not as representatives of Governments or countries. The publication of the Report does not imply that it necessarily represents the views of Commonwealth Governments, nor does it commit them individually or collectively to its recommendations.

In presenting the Report, the Group has expressed the hope that it will be of assistance in the preparations for the Special Session of the UN General Assembly in August-September 1980 on a New International Development Strategy for the 1980s and for the global round of negotiations which will follow. I share this hope, and have pleasure in making available through this Report the considered views of an independent group of Commonwealth experts as a contribution to the global dialogue.

**Shridath S Ramphal**

# Letter of Presentation

Marlborough House,
London, SW1Y 5HX.

4 June 1980.

H.E. Mr. S.S. Ramphal,
Commonwealth Secretary-General,
Marlborough House,
Pall Mall,
London, SW1.

Dear Secretary-General,

You appointed us as a group of independent experts from Commonwealth countries in accordance with paragraphs 42 and 43 of the Final Communique issued by Commonwealth Heads of Government after their meeting in Lusaka in August 1979.

As requested by that meeting, we herewith transmit to you our Report on the factors inhibiting structural change and a sustained improvement in economic growth, and on the specific measures by which developed and developing countries, Commonwealth and non-Commonwealth, might act to reduce or eliminate such constraints as a matter of urgency. We hope the Report will be useful in the preparation for the Special Session of the UN General Assembly in August-September 1980 on a new International Development Strategy for the 1980s and for the global round of negotiations which will follow.

As an independent group, we have signed the Report in our personal capacities and not as representatives of the Governments, countries or organisations to which we belong.

Please accept, Secretary-General, the expression of our highest consideration.

*H.W. Arndt*

*William G. Demas*

*A.D. Brownlie*

*Alec Cairncross*

*Lal Jayawardena*

*William Jenkins*

*Dominic C. Mulaisho*

*Ramon V. Navaratnam*

*H.M.A. Onitiri*

*Amartya Sen*

# Contents

# Preface

1. At their Lusaka meeting in August 1979, the Heads of Commonwealth Governments agreed to request the Secretary-General to commission an in-depth report by a group of eight to ten independent experts from Commonweath countries chosen from appropriate fields.

2. The Group's terms of reference were as follows:

> " . . . . . . . . . . . . . . . .to investigate and report on the factors inhibiting structural change and a sustained improvement in economic growth in both developed and developing countries, in particular the acceleration of growth in developing countries. The report, which should be clearly focused, should assess the importance of and the relationship between possible constraints, such as protection and adjustment policies, inflation, subsidies both on production and exports, fluctuations in commodity prices, availability and cost of energy resources, including oil, and factors inhibiting investment, transfer of technology and international flows of official and private resources".[1]

> " . . . . . . . . . . . . . . . .to identify specific measures by which developed and developing countries, Commonwealth and non-Commonwealth, might act to reduce or eliminate such constraints as a matter of urgency. They recognised that this would require attention at the highest political level. The group, which would be assembled by the Secretary-General after appropriate consultation with member Governments, should report in time to assist Commonwealth Governments in their preparation for the Special Session of the UN General Assembly in 1980".[2]

---

1. Commonwealth Heads of Government: *The Lusaka Communique*, paragraph 42 (Commonwealth Secretariat, London, 1979).

2. Ibid, paragraph 43.

3. The list of members of the Group is at Appendix 2.

4. The Group held three meetings in London in January, April and June 1980 and submitted its Report to the Commonwealth Secretary-General on 4 June 1980.

5. The Group, in preparing this Report, has had regard to several major developments since the Lusaka meeting of August 1979. These include:

(a) the publication of the Brandt Commission's report,[1] with its comprehensive treatment of some of the problems contained in the Group's terms of reference;

(b) further deepening of recession and slowdown of economic growth in some of the major countries of the OECD area than expected a year ago;

(c) a marked aggravation of balance of payments problems of oil-importing countries; and

(d) a deterioration in the atmosphere of *detente* between East and West.

The structure of the Report reflects at various points the emphasis which these developments lent to the Group's discussions.

6. In order to put the current problems in perspective we review the recent economic developments in Chapter 1 and draw attention to the relationship between the current crisis and the problems of poverty and starvation in the developing countries in Chapter 2. Chapter 3 deals with the problems of financing the balance of payments deficits of the developing countries. These problems have become so acute that unless new initiatives are taken urgently, many countries will find it impossible even to maintain their present income levels. This is followed in Chapter 4 by a discussion of the issues of protectionism and its adverse consequences for future development of the world economy. This is an area where positive action will be of great benefit to both the developed and the developing economies and will also contribute to lessening global inflationary pressures. In Chapter 5, we briefly consider the problem of inflation. This is followed by a consideration of energy issues, particularly the importance of accelerating exploration, the development of new energy resources, and conservation (Chapter 6). In Chapter 7, we have identified some other development issues which we believe have particular relevance to the present economic situation. Many of

---

1. Independent Commission on International Development Issues: *North-South: A Programme for Survival* (Pan Books, London, 1980).

the current problems are intimately related to problems of structural change. Measures to bring about such change, in our view, would also contribute to an acceleration of economic growth in both developed and developing countries. In Chapter 8, we summarise our main conclusions and stress the need for collective action to solve the present crisis. The world economy is now so interdependent that common economic problems can only be solved by concerted and mutually consistent action by all countries.

# 1. The Setting

1.1 As the world economy enters into the 1980s, there is considerable concern about its immediate future. Seldom have so many problems arisen at the same time. Economic growth has slowed down further and the industrialised countries appear to be on the threshold of a serious recession. Trade barriers, after a long period of liberalisation, have been raised on a number of critical exports. Meanwhile aid budgets are still very far from the agreed target. Oil prices have again increased sharply. Large debts have been incurred by parts of the Third World and there are doubts about the prospects for another round of massive 'recycling' through the international banks.

1.2 The current world economic crisis has its roots in the serious problems faced by the world economy since the beginning of the 1970s and, in some respects, even earlier. As economic growth slowed down, the world has found it increasingly difficult to deal with the tasks of containing inflation, maintaining full employment, sustaining development and alleviating poverty. It is the purpose of this chapter briefly to review the overall economic performance of the recent past in an attempt to provide a historical perspective for the problems which are undoubtedly interrelated and have led to the crisis described more fully in Chapter 2.

### Slow Growth and High Inflation

1.3 Throughout the 1970s rates of growth in the industrialised countries were on average substantially lower than in the 1960s. For the period 1970-1979 as a whole, the annual growth in output of the industrialised countries was about 3.4 per cent as against almost 4.8 per cent in the previous decade. The lower rate of growth resulted from attenuation in the 1970s of some of those factors which had promoted it actively in the 1950s and 1960s.[1]

1.4 Although the precise impact of individual factors is difficult to determine, the events that led to the slowing down of economic growth in industrialised countries are well known, and some of them go back to the 1960s. The breakdown of the Bretton Woods system in 1971 was a direct result of the loss of confidence in the dollar against the background of continuing massive United States external payments deficits. A high rate of monetary expansion in 1972-73 (facilitated by the absence of the usual balance of payments constraints) fed a commodity boom, on which was superimposed a series of agricultural harvest failures. The 1972-73 boom was exacerbated by the fact that supply bottlenecks appeared in response to rapidly rising inflation in many parts of the world. Prices of food, raw materials and industrial products all increased disproportionately compared with earlier upswings.

1.5 Inflation rose sharply in 1972-73. Fifteen years of relative price stability came to an end; Europe moved from inflation rates of under 5 per cent per year to over 10 per cent. The average rate of inflation in OECD countries more than doubled between the 1960s and 1970s. Unemployment rates also increased throughout the OECD area to levels unprecedented since World War II. The OECD has computed a crude 'discomfort index' (the sum of the rate of inflation and the rate of unemployment). This index rose from around 5½ percentage points in the 1960s to 17 percentage points in 1974-75. As Rostow puts it, there was a "convergence of stagnation and inflation unique in modern economic history".[2] Since then, inflation itself and concern to

1. Among the factors that have been noted in the economic literature as having contributed to post-war expansion in the world economy are: the primacy attached to economic growth as an objective of government policy; rapid technological change; growth in trade facilitated by a stable international monetary environment and reduction in tariff barriers; relatively cheap energy; labour migration to economies facing labour shortages; and substantial acceleration in the flow of capital, both governmental and private, from the developed to developing countries. See, for example, W.W. Rostow: *The World Economy: History and Prospect* (MacMillan, 1978); Interfutures: *Facing the Future* (OECD, Paris, 1979); H.W. Arndt: *The Rise and Fall of Economic Growth* (Longman, Cheshire, 1978); C.P. Kindleberger: *Europe's Post-war Growth* (Harvard University Press, 1967); World Bank: *World Development Report* (Washington, 1978); W. Kasper: 'Some Broad Perspectives of World Economic Growth', in W. Kasper and T.G. Parry: *Growth, Trade and Structural Change in an Open Australian Economy* (University of New South Wales, 1978).

2. W.W. Rostow, op. cit.

control inflation, have acted as a major constraint on any attempt to accelerate growth in most of the industrialised countries.

1.6 Inevitably these developments in the industrialised countries have adversely affected the economies of the developing countries. As noted by the World Bank, "with the collapse of a sustained and simultaneous boom in the industrialised countries, the peaking of major commodity prices and the sharp increase in the price of imported oil, 1974 marked a turning point in the economic performance and prospects of developing countries".[1] The effect of the recession in the industrialised countries, coming as it did on top of the energy crisis, was to lower growth rates of imports in the developing countries. The rate of growth of imports in these countries during 1974-1977 declined to 3.8 per cent per annum, which was almost half that in the previous ten years. Similarly, the growth of exports declined to a little over 4 per cent.

1.7 It is remarkable and encouraging that in these adverse circumstances, the growth performance of the Third World as a whole (even excluding the oil-producing countries of the Middle East and North Africa) stood up well. Growth rates of the middle-income countries, particularly those which had relied on trade as the primary engine of growth, declined somewhat but remained on average much higher than those of the OECD area. The low-income Asian countries even experienced a significant acceleration in their growth rates. Part of this improvement was due to better weather but there is some evidence that substantial investments made in the agricultural sector were beginning to yield results by the mid-1970s. The growth rates of the low-income countries as a group, however, have remained below those of the middle-income countries, and many of the least developed have suffered from continuing stagnation or in some cases even decline in per capita income.

1.8 Moreover, the record on redistribution, institutional reform and reduction in poverty levels in developing countries, with a few exceptions, was far from satisfactory. According to World Bank estimates, about 40 per cent of the population of developing countries are still living in 'absolute poverty'. The majority of them are in rural areas in the countries of South Asia, Indonesia, and sub-Saharan Africa. In addition to the absolute poor, large numbers of people have inadequate access to essential public services, such as health-care, safe drinking-water and sanitation. These include substantial proportions of the population in the middle-income countries. In the poorest countries, the incomes and consumption levels of the poorer half of the population have stagnated, and in countries where agriculture has expanded

1. World Bank: *World Development Report* (Washington, 1979).

more slowly than population (parts of South Asia and sub-Saharan Africa) the incomes of some of the rural population have probably declined. Unemployment and under-employment have continued to be acute in much of the developing world. Rapid urbanisation has created a variety of strains and social costs which have been evident in the growth of slums and shanty towns, in the pressing demand for schools and hospitals, and in the overloading of transport facilities. Some progress has been made in respect of education and health, but the deficiencies are many and the gaps in the availability of such basic facilities are still very wide, both among and within countries.

**Balance of Payments Deficits**

1.9 An important aspect of the post-1973 experience was the dramatic shift in the balance of payments positions of oil-exporting and oil-importing countries. The huge surpluses which resulted from the oil price increases in 1973 had their counterpart in large deficits in the oil-importing countries. The combined current account position of the OECD area, which had been in surplus in the 1960s and early 1970s, swung into a $33 billion deficit in 1974.[1] However, the deficit nearly vanished in the first half of 1975, as exports to OPEC countries rose sharply and recession brought a fall in imports by most oil-importing developed countries. The deficits subsequently widened again as OECD economic activity picked up, but by 1978 they had been, by and large, brought under control. The 1979 oil price increases once again raised the prospect of large deficits for the industrialised countries.

1.10 The experience of non-oil developing countries was more difficult. Their combined deficit increased in 1974 to almost three times the 1973 level of $ 11 billion. These deficits, although somewhat reduced in later years, remained high throughout 1974-1978. While the middle-income countries were generally able to finance even large and persistent deficits, some of them and most of the poorer developing countries suffered reductions, in real terms, in their import capacities and development expenditures. It is clear that many of the latter developing countries now require additional assistance on concessionary or grant terms if their economic development and even their current living standards are not to be depressed further.

1.11 Those countries which managed to maintain or even accelerate their imports and growth rates in the 1970s with the help of borrowings in international capital markets now find themselves with large accumulated debts. Not all of them may be able to continue borrowing on a substantial scale in

1. All figures in dollars in this Report refer to US dollars.

order to cover their newly enlarged deficits and maintain the momentum of their development. There is also doubt in some quarters, as discussed more fully in Chapter 3, about the capacity of international capital markets to recycle further large increases in OPEC surpluses.

**Future Prospects**

1.12 The problems of the 1970s look like becoming larger and more difficult in the 1980s.[1] As a result of the steep oil price increases of 1979 and inflation, growth in the OECD area as a whole is expected to decline sharply, from over 3 per cent in 1979 to 0.3 per cent in 1980.[2] Although no estimates are available for developing countries, their growth will almost certainly be damaged further by the increases in oil prices and the recession in the industrialised countries.

1.13 Since the Caracas meeting of OPEC in December 1979, estimates of the combined current account deficit of the OECD countries have been revised upwards to more than $75 billion, compared with $30 billion in 1979. Oil price rises, coupled with the effects of recession in the industrialised economies, will continue to aggravate the balance of payments problems of the net oil-importing developing countries. Towards the end of 1980, the combined current account deficit could be running at an annual average rate of $60-$70 billion. The average rate of inflation in the OECD countries is not expected to fall below the present level of 10 per cent while unemployment is likely to rise further.

1.14 The short-term problems could also complicate further the longer-term prospects. An OECD-commissioned report has referred to the danger of a 'low-growth trap', in which future recovery would be increasingly hampered by the lack of past investment because of monetary stringency and higher

1. For instance, the OECD Secretariat estimates that an increase of 10 per cent in oil prices in 1980 would affect the OECD's real output almost twice as much as an equivalent rise in 1979. This is mainly because (a) the net import bill of the OECD area is now larger, both in absolute terms and in relation to GNP; and (b) only about 15 per cent of any further increase in OPEC oil revenue, compared with about half of any such increase early in 1975, is likely to be spent within 12 months, as OPEC import volumes had already grown at a very rapid rate.

2. On the assumption that OPEC oil prices would remain unchanged in real terms after the increases announced up to November 1979, the OECD forecasts were for an overall 1 per cent growth rate in 1980; these were revised downward to virtual stagnation after the increases announced towards the end of 1979.

interest rates.[1] It stresses the need for positive help on the supply side. This involves encouraging structural adjustment and concentrating state aid on industries with fair medium-term prospects. Effective energy policies remain, however, a key element in this structural investment approach. And the fact that demand for energy has been reduced by recession should not lead to complacency about the urgency with which these policies need to be pursued.

1.15 The experience of the 1970s suggests that the continuation of slow growth, the difficulties in bringing down inflation and the balance of payments constraints have been due to deep-seated changes, involving structural causes which limit the use and adequacy of growth policies as they have been pursued in the past. The work of the Interfutures Group[2] has identified at least three types of structural constraints on governments' ability to accelerate growth in industrialised countries: (a) those which relate to the 'crumbling of the social consensus' within the industrialised societies, leading to persistent inflationary expectations and structural unemployment; (b) those which result from the fact that the industrialised world has become, with the relative decline of the USA and an increase in the importance of Japan and Western Europe, a multipolar one, particularly in the monetary, trade and technology spheres; and (c) those which reflect the increased importance of international as opposed to domestic demand. This, together with the increased political awareness of and disparities within the Third World, has brought about extremely important changes in relations between the developed and the developing world.

1.16 One result of these constraints is, perhaps, a lower degree of effectiveness of purely national macro-economic policies. Yet, they have led to more defensive national action as governments have perceived a greater vulnerability of their domestic economies. For example, when governments seek to protect existing industries and jobs, it almost certainly has the effect of putting a further brake on economic growth and thus serving to increase rather than reduce unemployment. An alternative, and undoubtedly more effective response, would have been to adopt a collective approach to overcoming these constraints.

1.17 The 1970s have also demonstrated that the adverse effects of slow growth in industrialised countries on the economies of developing countries must be taken into account in the mutual interest of both groups of countries.

---

1. Interfutures, op. cit.

2. *Towards full employment and price stability* (a report to the OECD by a group of independent experts headed by Paul McCracken), (OECD, Paris, June 1977).

Moreover, this mutuality of interest has to be realised in the context of longer-term structural problems within the developed and developing countries as well as that of the changing relationships between the two groups. In short, while slow growth makes it difficult to bring about structural changes, higher growth cannot be sustained without them.

# 2. Development and Crisis

2.1 Development efforts in the past few decades have had considerable success. Few developing countries stand today where they did after the second world war, and some have achieved remarkably fast rates of growth. Despite these achievements, there is a strong sense of economic crisis in the developing world today. Partly, this is a reflection of the current international recession which has made the development efforts of all countries harder and which has begun to have devastating effects on some of them. But aside from these recessionary problems and the particular difficulties caused by the energy crisis, there are also deep-rooted structural problems which add to political and economic concerns. It is recognised that there has been a widespread failure to realise the much desired objectives enshrined in programmes of successive development decades. Part of the disquiet arises from these long-run failures, and especially from the inability of the world economic structure – with its inequalities and asymmetries – to come into equilibrium with the changed political structure arising from the emergence of the colonial peoples into politically independent nations. The contrast between expectations and achievements provides a sombre backdrop to the current economic crisis.

2.2 Eradication of poverty has been a major international preoccupation in the changed political situation after the second world war. During the 1950s and 1960s the fast expansion of the world economy held up the hope that the more acute problems of the developing countries might disappear through sharing this rapid economic growth. This has not happened. First, the expansion of the world economy has not been sustained in the 1970s and there has been a deepening of recession recently. Second, even when the expansion of the world economy was fast and some particular developing countries fully shared in this rapid growth, it failed to carry with it many other developing countries. Finally, even in some developing countries that did grow fast, the poverty problem did not get substantially reduced, partly because of growing inequality. While this last is largely a matter for the internal policy of developing countries, pointing to a need for institutional changes within their economies, the widespread failure of developing countries to share in economic growth has brought into question the efficiency and justice of the existing economic order in the world. It has contributed to Third World demands for a new international economic order and for corresponding structural changes in international economic relations. The existing international order has, however, proved resistant to change, and the present crisis has occurred in a world economy that was already in difficulties despite high average growth rates in the 1960s.

2.3 In this context, it is also important to examine the exceptional vulnerability of substantial sections of the population within the poorer economies to any economic deterioration. The poorer sections of the population in developing countries live precariously close to starvation, and even a relatively small decline in their economic position can push them into it. There is, in fact, evidence that much starvation, and even many of the major famines in this century, have taken place in good food availability situations, and hunger has been caused not by a fall in food supply, but by a sharp decline in the so-called 'economic entitlements' of substantial sections of the population.[1] Economic entitlements of a family refer to goods and services over which that family can establish command through the economic, political and legal mechanisms in operation in that country. A peasant who grows his own food is entitled to that food without having to buy it in the market. But the question of incomes and prices is crucial for others who do not grow food (e.g. craftsmen, urban labourers), or who do not own the food they grow (e.g. agricultural wage labourers), or who have to sell substantial parts of their output of superior food to buy larger amounts of cheaper calories (e.g. fishermen or herdsmen having to exchange fish or animals for foodgrain). The overall availability of food is only one factor among many which influence the food entitlements of each section of the community. An economic crisis leading to substantial unemployment in a country without social security in general and unemployment benefits in particular, can precipitate starvation through lack of income to buy food, even when food supply is completely unaffected. So can sudden changes in relative prices and other parameters of economic entitlement.

2.4 In understanding the problems created by the current crisis in the world

---

1. For a study of these issues, prepared for the ILO World Employment Programme, see A.K. Sen: *Poverty and Famine: An Essay on Entitlement and Deprivation* (Oxford University Press, 1980).

economy, we have to take note both of the special difficulties of the developing economies in the unreformed international economic order *and* of the special vulnerability of wide sections of the population in the developing countries to economic fluctuations. The former aspect of the problem has been much discussed recently, and we are in sympathy with the analysis of world economic problems in the McIntyre Group's report[1] and in the Brandt Commission's report.[2] The latter aspect has, however, received less attention than is justified, and the seriousness of the economic dangers facing the developing world has been frequently underestimated.

2.5 The possibility of a world food crisis has recently been widely discussed. The importance of expanding world food output has been rightly stressed, especially in view of the problems created by the rise in the price of fertilisers linked with the energy crisis. Current trends, however, do not yet show world food supply lagging behind population growth, and a single-minded concern with the ratio of population to food may have the effect of blinding the world community to the real immediate dangers that face the developing economies. The fact that large-scale starvation is associated with *economic* fluctuations, which are not always accompanied by fluctuations of food supply, is the important point to keep in sight in analysing the current economic crisis. The international recession can lead to widespread starvation even without a food crisis as such.

2.6 The balance of payments problems created by the energy situation have received attention, since it has become increasingly difficult for net oil-importing developing countries to meet their import bills. However, from an economic – rather than a narrowly defined trade – point of view, there are two additional aspects of the problem. The first is the obvious one that the rise in energy costs is more than a payments problem for energy-deficient countries; it amounts to a decline in real income, and for countries that are already poor, this can be particularly serious. The less obvious but no less important point concerns the question of vulnerability of entitlements. The payments crisis as well as the real income effect of the rise in energy costs may lead to a sudden and sharp contraction in certain sections of the economy of developing countries. Those whose livelihood depends on economic activity in these sections will then suddenly find their occupation gone, and income too. If the economy were buoyant, they could get other gainful occupations, but these economies are not at present buoyant. If an adequate

1. A final report by a Commonwealth Experts' Group: *Towards a New International Economic Order* (Commonwealth Secretariat, London, 1977).

2. Independent Commission on International Development Issues, op. cit.

system of social security were in operation in the developing countries, the economic problems of the displaced people would be partially compensated, but for various obvious reasons, social security is typically absent in the poorer developing countries. Of such situations, starvation is born.

2.7 Again, there is an important asymmetry between unemployment problems in the developed countries and those in most of the developing ones. In the former, unemployment precipitates suffering, but – given the system of social security – very rarely leads to starvation. Not so in the developing economies. This sharp contrast has to be borne in mind in understanding the problems created by different aspects of the current world economic crisis. The balance of payments difficulties created both by the slowdown in the growth rates of the OECD countries and by the rise in energy costs threaten the developing world with accentuation of poverty in general and widespread starvation in particular. The urgency of devising ways and means of preventing sudden contractions in the developing economies which could have such disastrous effects must, therefore, be viewed in more specific terms than provided by the aggregate statistics of stagnation and sluggish performance. For example, when in Chapter 3 we discuss schemes for international lending and 'recycling' of funds to avoid a sudden economic contraction, we are talking also about starvation and not only about the level of economic activity.

2.8 The same issue is present in the analysis of protectionism in the developed economic world. While the object of such protectionism is to shield the workers in particular sectors of the developed countries from the dole queues (that object may or may not in fact be realised by protectionism), the consequence may be to push craftsmen and labourers in the corresponding sections of the developing countries to acute misery and starvation, without encountering any dole queues since there are no doles.

2.9 The focus on entitlement vulnerability also permits a fuller appreciation of the dangers of exporting inflation. Starvation can be caused not merely by unemployment, but also by a shift in relative prices of other goods vis-a-vis food, and indeed severe starvation – even famine – has been caused in the past by such shifts in relative prices. One of the more alarming aspects of inflation is that it leads to sharp changes in relative prices, and this can precipitate starvation even without any decline in food supply and even without much unemployment. The fact that the current world economic crisis has led to the exporting of *both* unemployment and inflation, thus makes it urgent for us to view it especially in the perspective of the variability of economic entitlements.

2.10 The contrast between different developing countries becomes relevant in this context also. Some of them are rich enough to have a cushion between typical earnings and acute poverty, though even in many of the richer developing countries starvation still does take place among the more vulnerable sections of the population when a sudden economic crisis occurs. Some other developing countries (for example Sri Lanka), while not particularly rich, have found it possible to provide a modicum of social security (for example in the form of free distribution of some food rations), and have been able to lessen the problem of vulnerability to economic crisis. But for the bulk of the developing countries the problem of starvation and acute poverty is present, and is liable to be devastatingly intensified by economic fluctuations.

2.11 Even those developing countries which are fairly immune from the problem of starvation as such have other areas of vulnerability in facing the current international crisis. The balance of payments problems can lead to the collapse of development efforts, making the already hard battle against underdevelopment that much harder still. The dampening effects of energy shortage as well as of protectionism in the developed world market can have severe destabilizing effects on earnings, employment, investment and consumption. The specific problems to which much of this Report is devoted can be seen in their proper perspective only when the background – outlined above – is kept in view. In that background lies much economic vulnerability, much frustration with the international order, and much gap between expectations and achievements.

2.12 Finally, while the economic problems are substantially more acute in the developing countries than in the developed ones, the extent of misery caused by the present crisis even in the developed economies must not be underestimated. With severe (in some cases, unprecedented) unemployment, acute inflation and deepening recession, substantial sections of the population of the richer countries have also been plunged into economic deprivation and suffering. While the nature and seriousness of the problems as well as their genesis vary from country to country, there are enough threats in common to call for an international programme of concerted action. To the requirements of such a programme we now turn.

# 3. The Balance of Payments Problem

3.1 It is a truism that the sum of the balance of payments surpluses and deficits on the current account of all countries must be zero. In other words, when there are current account surpluses (such as those run by OPEC today), there are counterpart deficits that will have been financed and which exactly equal the surpluses. This equality obtains *ex-post* in any single year's accounting; in fact, it only indicates that the surpluses will have been lent or 'recycled' to finance the deficits that actually occur.

3.2 These deficits will be diminished if the surplus countries can expand their imports either by boosting domestic activity or by allowing their rates of exchange to appreciate. But if there is no such relief to the strain on the financing mechanism, and if the mechanism is ineffective in permitting deficit countries to obtain finance from abroad, adjustment can take place only through a decline in economic activity, concentrated on the deficit countries but reacting throughout the system and bringing about an all-round curtailment of trade. The system will settle in balance at whatever level is required to balance the surpluses with the deficits that can be financed.

3.3 In the 1970s, all these three processes, the lending of surpluses, the increase of imports into the surplus countries, and a reduction in the level of economic activity, were at work. OPEC surpluses after 1973 were run down more rapidly than expected because of high imports. In 1973, total OPEC surpluses had been about $5 billion. They then shot up to $64 billion in 1974, but declined to $24 billion in 1977 and were almost zero in 1978. This decline, to a significant extent, was due to a very rapid expansion in the imports of OPEC countries.

3.4 At the same time, there was a substantial increase in bank lending to developing countries. This facilitated the financing of deficits. The developing countries' debt outstanding in the financial markets increased from over $ 30 billion in 1974 to about $ 100 billion in 1979, with the result that commercial banks' lending became the largest single component in the flow of funds. Official development assistance and the IMF played a diminishing role in financing the deficits: only about 6 per cent of the current account deficit of non-oil developing countries was financed by the IMF in 1974. It made a negative contribution, with repurchases exceeding drawings, during 1977-1979.

3.5 To the extent to which the financing mechanism did not work and imports into surplus countries did not increase, what inevitably occurred was a contraction in economic activity. This was particularly true of those developing countries which did not have sufficient resilience to increase substantially their exports or were not considered to be sufficiently creditworthy to increase their borrowings from commercial banks.

**Prospects for the Early 1980s**

3.6 There is a danger that, without corrective policy action, more of the adjustment to balance of payments difficulties in the 1980s will be brought about through reduction in the level of economic activity than through the on-lending of surpluses or through increases in imports of surplus countries. First, the magnitude of the problem is substantially larger now than in the past. Present projections suggest an OPEC surplus on current account of well over $100 billion in 1980 and a further substantial increase in 1981. Some long-term forecasts suggest a cumulative surplus for OPEC of $400 billion between 1979 and 1983 as compared with about $150 billion during 1974-1978. Second, apart from the expected persistence of surpluses, there is a real fear now being voiced by private banks that they cannot cope with the recycling problem. The banks are becoming increasingly cautious in overextending their exposure to the small group of countries which account for the bulk of the borrowings. This caution is reflected in a decline since 1977 in the rate of expansion of bank lending to developing countries. The banks are also becoming concerned about the adequacy of their capital in relation to the total size of deposits. Third, the absorptive capacity of OPEC for additional imports appears to be much less now than in the 1970s. Fourth, an important element which moderated the recessionary trend during the 1970s appears to be absent. Many of the developed countries which pursued expansionary policies then are not doing so now. This is specially true of the United States, the United Kingdom and Italy where the real and understandable concern with inflation has meant the adoption of restrictive domestic policies.

3.7 Much will depend on the policies pursued by the developed countries which will feel the main impact of higher oil prices. The combined deficit on current account of the OECD countries is expected to increase from $30 billion in 1979 to about $75 billion in 1980. This swing looks like being heavily concentrated on Germany and Japan and may continue into 1981. Both of these countries are in a strong position to run large deficits with equanimity if they so decide; but if they were to allow domestic activity to slow down or contract in an effort to reduce these deficits, or if they improved their balance of payments substantially by a highly successful export drive, a general contraction in world economic activity would be difficult to avoid.

3.8 The net oil-importing developing countries face equally difficult balance of payments problems which would be greatly intensified by any failure on the part of the developed countries to sustain activity. Higher oil prices alone may add some $ 24 billion to their collective import bill in 1980, compared with 1978. This comes on top of adjustments which most of the developing countries have had to make since 1973 through a sharp compression in imports, a fall in growth rates, and a substantial cut-back in development expenditure.

3.9 Estimates of the current account for the group of *net* oil-importing developing countries have been made by the IMF and show an increase in their deficit from $29 billion in 1978 to $46 billion in 1979 and a forecast of $62 billion for 1980.[1] These figures compare with a deficit of only $9 billion in 1973, a favourable year. When account is taken of official aid and capital inflows, however, these deficits disappear and the IMF calculations show a net surplus for the balance of payments as a whole of $15 billion in 1978, $9 billion in 1979 and a forecast for 1980 of $2 billion (see Table 3.1). On this showing there might seem to be very little to worry about.

3.10 The picture is, however, very different for the different sub-groups of countries making up the total. The developing countries which rank as major exporters of manufactures have run a considerable annual deficit on current account throughout the 1970s but have usually been able to cover it with something to spare through a large net inflow of capital. It is these countries which account for a large part of the oil-imports of developing countries and for most of the inflow of commercial banking funds, almost 80 per cent of private bank lending during the 1970s going to countries in this sub-group. If, as the IMF forecasts, they run a current account deficit in 1980 of $25-$30 billion this will be by no means easy to finance. It is true that most of

1. For *all* non-oil developing countries the current account deficit in 1979 is estimated at $54 billion, rising to $68 billion in 1980 and $78 billion in 1981.

**TABLE 3.1**
**Net Oil-importing Developing Countries**
**Summary of Balances of Payments, 1973 and 1978-80**
**(billion US dollars)**

| | 1973 | 1978 | 1979 | 1980 |
|---|---|---|---|---|
| Net oil-importing countries | | | | |
| Exports (f.o.b.) | 71.3 | 158.2 | 195.2 | 235.4 |
| Imports (f.o.b.) | –80.8 | –185.1 | –237.2 | –291.2 |
| Trade balance | –9.5 | –26.9 | –42.1 | –55.8 |
| Net services & private transfers | 0.8 | –1.9 | –4.0 | –5.9 |
| Balance on current account | –8.7 | –28.8 | –46.1 | –61.7 |
| Net official transfers | 3.3 | 5.8 | 8.8 | 9.3 |
| Net capital inflows | 13.6 | 38.2 | 46.4 | 54.3 |
| Overall balance[3] | 8.2 | 15.2 | 9.1 | 1.9 |
| Of which : | | | | |
| 1. Major exporters of manufactures[1] | | | | |
| Imports (f.o.b.) | –48.5 | –109.6 | –144.3 | –179.4 |
| Balance on current account | –4.0 | –8.3 | –18.0 | –27.6 |
| Net capital inflows | 8.6 | 18.7 | 23.6 | 27.5 |
| Overall balance[3] | 5.6 | 11.6 | 8.3 | 2.8 |
| 2. Low-income countries[2] | | | | |
| Imports (f.o.b.) | –8.3 | –17.2 | –20.4 | –24.9 |
| Balance on current account | –3.4 | –7.3 | –9.1 | –10.8 |
| Net official transfers | 1.3 | 2.4 | 2.8 | 3.1 |
| Net capital inflows | 2.4 | 4.7 | 6.3 | 6.1 |
| Overall balance[3] | 0.3 | –0.2 | – | –1.6 |
| 3. All other countries | | | | |
| Imports (f.o.b.) | –24.0 | –58.1 | –72.3 | –86.9 |
| Balance on current account | –1.3 | –13.0 | –17.2 | –23.4 |
| Net capital inflows | 2.5 | 14.7 | 16.5 | 20.7 |
| Overall balance[3] | 2.2 | 3.6 | 2.6 | 0.7 |

Source: International Monetary Fund.

1. Includes Argentina, Brazil, Republic of China (Taiwan), Greece, Hong Kong, India, Israel, Korea, Portugal, Singapore, South Africa and Yugoslavia.
2. Thirty-eight countries with a per capita income of below US $300 in 1977. India, which is also a low-income country, is included in the group of major exporters of manufactures.
3. Includes net official transfers.

them enjoy a high credit-rating in the international capital market but this does not mean that they can borrow what they choose, particularly if the economic climate continues to deteriorate. Anxiety currently being expressed about over-exposure of the banking system may well limit the additions they can make to their borrowings. There is also no guarantee that what they raise abroad for domestic investment will match their balance of payments deficit over the same period. In general, however, any residual financing difficulties experienced by countries in this sub-group should be capable of being met by recourse to the IMF through transitional facilities there and on acceptable conditions.[1]

3.11 It is otherwise with two other sub-groups: the low-income countries (with a per capita income below $300 in 1977) and an intermediate group of countries which are mainly primary producers. Their current account deficits have increased steadily and are unlikely to be financed from available sources. Moreover, the structural rigidities in their economies imply the need for substantially longer-term programme financing beyond that available through the IMF. The first of the two sub-groups is the more vulnerable. Their import volumes have scarcely grown in real terms since 1972. The real purchasing power of their exports has declined significantly. Import volumes have in these circumstances been maintained by current balance of payment deficits that are large in relation to imports – nearly 45 per cent in 1979, as compared with 15 per cent for the major exporters of manufactures and 27 per cent for 'other' net importers of oil. In contrast to these other sub-groups of countries, private bank financing of the deficits of the low-income developing countries has been largely absent, and the burden has been carried by official sources. It is not surprising, therefore, that the balance of payments out-turn for 1980, as projected by the IMF, implies a continuing stagnation in their import volumes. Even so, on this assumption there will be an increase in their 1980 current account deficit as compared with 1979 of about $1.5 billion, with another $1 billion increment projected in 1981.

3.12 While this sub-group consumes and imports significantly less oil than other sub-groups of developing countries, their total oil-import bill was roughly $2.5 billion in 1979 and the increment resulting from the price developments of 1979 may be around $2 billion. Additional finance on at least this scale will have to be found from non-commercial sources if these countries are not to fall further behind.

---

1. The argument of this paragraph is not intended to apply to India which is more appropriately grouped with low-income and residual countries discussed below.

3.13 The residual category of nearly 50 other net oil-importing developing countries has a degree of resilience to external shocks intermediate between that of the low-income countries and the major exporters of manufactures. Their prospective deficit on current account shows a rise from $13 billion in 1978 to over $23 billion in 1980. While the IMF projections for their balance of payments as a whole indicate a barely positive surplus of less than $1 billion, this could readily be transformed into a deficit falling on reserves if the assumptions underlying the calculation go awry in the course of the year.

3.14 In summary, then, the 1980 picture that emerges for the net oil-importing developing countries is that while the major exporters of manufactures may be able to cope with varying degrees of difficulty within the existing sources of finance available to them, the remaining categories, namely the low-income countries and the residual category of middle-income primary producers, are likely to require additional support over at least the next two years. Certainly, all of them would require financing extending beyond the traditional time-frame of IMF facilities, though the more diversified economies among them can for the present look to the IMF through transitional facilities there on appropriate terms and conditions. For 1981, all countries would be vulnerable – the IMF forecasts an incremental deficit of $10 billion over the 1980 figure without providing any indication of how this increment might be financed.

3.15 A broadly similar assessment was expressed to the IMF's Interim Committee by its Managing Director Mr. de Larosiere on 25 April 1980, especially with respect to the difficulties lying ahead for 1980 and the need for longer-term programme financing. Having argued that while "the outlook for 1980 with respect to the financing of balance of payments imbalances is reasonably reassuring", he went on to say that this

> "was not a reason for complacency. The expected further increase in the current account deficit of the non-oil LDCs in 1981, coupled with virtual stagnation in the volume of import growth, foreshadows a very difficult situation. Indeed, even now there are some warning signals in the financial markets: an increase in spreads, a shortening of maturities, and greater selectivity exercised by commercial banks in taking up new risks. And the signals suggest that banks might become more cautious in the recycling process as time goes by, and perhaps less active in this very essential intermediation function."[1]

---

1. IMF: *World Economic Outlook and the Role of the Fund in Payments Adjustment and Financing,* page 3.

## Immediate Balance of Payments Needs

3.16 It is not possible to arrive at a precise measure of the additional support required in 1980 and 1981 by the low-income and residual category of developing countries. The more aid they receive, the less it will be necessary for them to react to less favourable terms of trade in ways that involve still further impoverishment. One measure of what they might reasonably seek in aid or additional support would be the increase in their import bill for oil which in 1980 is likely to be around $10 billion. But this understates the strain on their balance of payments occasioned by higher oil prices, since the disruption in world markets reacts back on the demand for their exports. As shown in Table 3.1, the current account of these two sub-groups of developing countries deteriorated by $6 billion in 1979 and may deteriorate by a further $8 billion in 1980. This suggests that the IMF's estimate of the overall balance of payments for these countries may be somewhat optimistic. Given the large increase in the import bill for oil and the still larger deterioration in the current account, additional support on the scale of at least $5 billion a year, and possibly $10 billion a year, might be necessary to preserve the levels of income of two years ago.

3.17 To this must be added further aid to assist in the process of structural adjustment to higher energy prices. Unless the additional aid on balance of payments grounds is to continue indefinitely, or its discontinuance is to plunge the poorer countries into just those depths of poverty which it was designed to avoid, a beginning will have to be made with longer-term adjustments in the economy to the change in the terms of trade and the balance of payments. These may be such as to effect economies in the use of imported oil or make for an expansion of exports or a curtailment of imports in other ways. They are not likely to be accomplished without investment and the funds required may have to come to a large extent from foreign aid. Thus the immediate need for balance of payments support shades into the need to bring about structural adjustments to a balance of payments problem that has become more acute, and this in turn leads on to the need for other long-term structural change in the interests of economic development. To set on foot projects that help to reduce a continuing balance of payments deficit requires longer-term programme finance, extending over the period of gestation of the projects, than is needed in situations where the deficit can be expected to reverse itself in, say, three to five years.

3.18 Against this background we have considered what action might be taken to ease the problems of the developing countries and so contribute to greater stability in international trade and economic activity generally. Since it would be unrealistic to expect an increase in imports into the surplus

(OPEC) countries in the short-run or the injection of an expansionary bias in developed countries gripped with inflation, that leaves only one area of effective policy action. It is to find ways to provide additional financing mechanisms, both through commercial banks and through governmental channels, to meet deficits in order to sustain economic activity on acceptable terms.

3.19 Over the next year or two it will not be easy to add to those mechanisms in ways that provide balance of payments support of the order of $5-$10 billion (additional to the aid and capital inflows already assumed in paragraph 3.16). There is scope for additional bilateral aid and for a larger element of grant or interest subsidy in the aid supplied. Substantial additional help may come from the OPEC Special Fund. It should be possible for the IBRD to make fuller use of programme lending to those countries even within the limits to which its operations have hitherto been confined. It should also be possible for the IMF to establish a new facility, along the lines suggested below, which would lend to the poorer developing countries on first credit tranche conditions. But for the least developed countries and some other lower income countries whose debt situation is already serious, resort to the IMF except on very favourable terms offers little help. Many of these countries cannot afford to incur additional debt even on Third Window terms (i.e. 4 per cent interest and 25 years maturity) and need grants or soft IDA-type financing. For some of them it will be necessary to reschedule their debts. For nearly all of them the need is for a special programme of increased bilateral and multilateral assistance for the next few years, and efforts should be directed urgently to arrangements for this purpose.

3.20 In the longer run, other financing mechanisms could be devised. The large OPEC surpluses open up new possibilities. They create the danger of massive exchange instability, but the provision of satisfactory assets to remove this danger could take place in ways making it easier to engage in longer-term borrowing in order to effect structural adjustments in the developing countries. The crux of the problem from the OPEC point of view is that higher oil revenues will increase the OPEC holdings of foreign exchange by a large amount in relation to their existing stock of foreign exchange. In the single year 1980, the banks are expected to receive a flow of funds from OPEC countries ranging from $30 billion to $50 billion compared with the stock of $87 billion that OPEC had placed with them by the middle of 1979. There are serious doubts whether the markets are capable of handling such a large and sudden increment in the existing stock, without causing exchange rate instability. Funds are likely to move rapidly from one asset to another as depositors seek to diversify the composition of their reserve portfolios.

3.21 If this situation is to be avoided, policy action directed towards achieving the following objectives is now necessary:

(a) the prevention of potential exchange rate instability by ensuring that sufficiently attractive long-term reserve assets are available to OPEC countries;

(b) the establishment of a mechanism or mechanisms to facilitate larger flows of commercial funds to net oil-importing developing countries; and

(c) an increase in the availability of official sources of financing for countries which are not in a position to borrow from the commercial banks.

3.22 The policy action we suggest could be taken in a series of steps in financial intermediation, which would aim to provide funds both for balance of payments support and for the financing of structural adjustments to balance of payments difficulties. This action would necessarily take some time but could result in more satisfactory and longer-term arrangements than those that can be contrived with existing financing mechanisms.

3.23 First, comes the need to provide facilities to diversify the reserves of oil producers through off-market transactions with central banks. Alternatively, the same results could be achieved through a negotiated dollar Substitution Account within the IMF. If the IMF does not operate such an account there is all the more need for it to take advantage of other mechanisms of reserve diversification in order to 'recycle' the funds that can come to it via central banks. Second, the negotiating sequence that we propose would leave central banks in possession of dollars that could be re-lent to developing countries on longer-term within a suitable financing framework. The third step is the establishment of a mechanism that would put such re-lending on a genuinely long-term basis for programme financing purposes. This mechanism would build on the framework of central bank cooperation through the negotiation of guarantee arrangements between governments. Bonds would be floated against these guarantees and included in these issues would be bonds issued to subscribers of funds derived from off-market diversification arrangements. Finally, this mechanism could be given permanent institutional form by converting the guarantees into the callable capital (in the sense of a system of 'limited and several guarantees') of a lending institution such as the World Development Fund proposed by the Brandt Commission.

3.24 In so far as they meet both programme and project financing needs, proposals along these lines are developed in Appendix 1 and seem to us to merit consideration. We content ourselves here with an outline of those features of the proposals that seem to us crucial.

**Reserve Diversification**

3.25 The first step would consist in providing facilities for off-market reserve diversification by oil producers in order to reduce exchange rate instability caused by switches of their reserve assets between currencies while preventing unwanted changes in the money supply of the countries affected. In practice, these facilities would have to be such as to allow oil producers to unload dollars without undue disturbance to dollar exchange rates and receive in return assets denominated in some preferred currency. The off-market transactions involved would require to be negotiated among the central banks of the countries concerned and would, in the first instance, have the effect of creating a tier of secondary reserve assets for the participating central banks.

3.26 Such a negotiating sequence might proceed, illustratively, as follows: the Saudi Arabian Monetary Authority (SAMA) would sell the dollars received for its oil to the German Bundesbank in exchange for securities denominated in Deutsche Mark. These securities would represent secondary reserve assets for the SAMA whose terms as regards interest rate, maturity, etc. would be negotiated at somewhat *below* market rates, to reflect some sharing of the exchange risk being borne by the Bundesbank in selling Deutsche Mark securities for dollars.

3.27 The circuit would be completed by the Bundesbank investing the dollars so acquired in the United States in dollar-denominated bonds on terms negotiated *above* market rates, thus permitting the Bundesbank to share some of the remaining exchange risk with the United States. This type of negotiating sequence has a precedent in the two-year Roosa bonds negotiated in the middle 1960s to relieve pressure on the US dollar. Indeed, this process has already been set in train as a result of recent transactions between the Bundesbank and the SAMA and projected similar transactions involving the latter and the Bank of Japan. The issue of securities by the Bundesbank, however, has so far been limited to amounts required towards financing the Federal Republic's budget deficit without any rise in domestic interest rates. If there were a willingness to extend further the reserve role of the Deutsche Mark, then one could envisage additional transactions between the Bundesbank and the SAMA that would lead to the Bundesbank investing the dollars so acquired in the United States and completing the sequence previously described.

3.28 The principal innovative feature of this type of negotiating sequence is that it can enable monies to be lent to developing countries as well. For the dollars which find a home in the United States at the end of the negotiating circuit could be re-lent to developing countries within, of course, a framework of suitable terms and conditions for financing their deficits. Specifically, the Federal Reserve Board which would have received the dollars would make them available to the IMF against IMF obligations denominated preferably in SDRs or in dollars, somewhat in the manner in which finance was obtained for the IMF's 'oil' facility in the 1970s. As in the 1970s, the need to await the development of mechanisms described below for longer-term financing of deficits would mean that the amounts to be re-lent to developing countries within the framework of traditional IMF facilities would have to be on a broadly similar basis of conditionality to that of the 'oil' facility – viz. first credit tranche. Action to enable recycling via the IMF would constitute the second step in the series we recommend. Given the amounts requiring to be negotiated for reserve diversification purposes in the early 1980s, this form of re-lending could be the nucleus of a 'massive recycling process'.

3.29 In principle the same results in terms of both diversification and recycling can be achieved through a negotiated dollar Substitution Account within the IMF. This is simpler because it avoids a multiplicity of bilateral transactions among the central banks concerned. The case for such a Substitution Account has been urged by the Witteveen Group of Thirty.[1] But it has to be recognised that, considering the time it will take to put the Substitution Account into place, and granted the likely strength of desire for diversification of currency reserves, cooperation among central banks will be required. The case for such cooperation is further strengthened by the postponement within the IMF of the Substitution Account issue at the recent Hamburg meeting of the IMF Interim Committee. Indeed, the Witteveen Group has referred to one such form of central bank cooperation as 'the foreign currency substitution channel', in terms which make it virtually equivalent to the negotiating sequence which we have described, with the difference that in their formulation no explicit provision is made for re-lending and recycling the amount to the developing countries.[2]

---

1. The Reserve Assets Study Group of the Group of Thirty: *Reserve Assets and A Substitution Account: Towards a Less Unstable International Monetary System*, February 1980, page 10.

2. See ibid., page 18: "An alternative or complementary approach to the balance of payments channel is the foreign currency substitution channel. Problems posed by the relative lack of development of surplus countries' capital markets might also, to some extent, be avoided by this approach

*continued*

3.30 The advantage of adopting the route of negotiated off-market reserve diversification is that transfers to developing countries can be grafted on to the meeting of urgently felt central bank needs on which rapid action is bound to result, in response to market pressures. In the short-run, however, since the securities that will have to be negotiated among central banks are in the nature of secondary reserve assets, they are likely to be of a relatively short-term nature. The negotiation of terms which involves a sharing-out of the exchange risk between three or more parties will not be an easy matter. There may not be much room for manoeuvre, initially, therefore, regarding the maturity for re-lending the amounts to developing countries. Hence the short-run plausibility of the suggestion that the IMF become the intermediary for channelling these funds to developing countries.

3.31 A clear distinction will have to be drawn between funds disbursed through the existing facilities of the IMF to meet immediate needs for financing of balance of payments deficits and those earmarked for some new and longer-term 'oil' or structural change mechanism still to be set up. There is a need for resources for both purposes.

3.32 The resources available for the IMF's current facilities comprise about $10 billion worth of lendable currencies and another $10 billion from the Supplementary Financing Facility (the Witteveen facility), of which more than half will have been committed under ongoing negotiations. Although the high degree of conditionality attached to existing IMF facilities, in particular the Supplementary Financing Facility, inhibits recourse to them, increasing calls are likely to be made on these facilities by the developed countries and the first sub-group of developing countries (the major exporters

---

2. *Continued*
which allows for diversificaton outside the markets. For example, the strong currency countries could issue obligations in their own currencies in exchange for dollar claims on the United States. The advantage would be that they could thereby arguably sterilise the domestic monetary effects of foreign currency inflows before they actually occurred; that such techniques would be independent of the state of the countries' domestic financial markets; and that if the claims were in the form of long-term placements with central banks, they could be less volatile than short-term capital inflows. This approach might be considered analogous to a swap, with one leg of it in longer-term assets. However, strong currency countries would under this proposal have to accept further accumulations of dollar reserves and presumably the resultant exchange risk, unless bilateral arrangements are agreed between participating countries to share the exchange risk or the strong currency countries deposited newly-acquired dollar reserves in the Substitution Account."

of manufactures) discussed above. If the IMF's existing resources prove inadequate they could readily be supplemented, especially since the relatively short-term nature of the assets intitially generated in the course of off-market diversification transactions make them a permissible and attractive form of replenishment of IMF resources.

3.33 The Minister of Development Cooperation of the Netherlands has recently proposed that

> "In concrete terms, the IMF could use funds drawn from the capital market to finance the balance of payments deficits of the oil-importing developing countries on a medium-term or long-term basis. Short-term financing would be pointless in view of the structural nature of the deficits. . . . So my first proposal is to establish a new mode of operation by having the IMF borrow on the capital market to finance the deficits of the oil-importing developing countries."[1]

From one point of view this is a highly attractive proposal and has the great merit of simplicity. However, a genuine question arises as to how far recycling through the IMF to developing countries could be sustained over a period of years on a sufficiently longer-term basis in line with the structural nature of the deficits requiring to be financed. It is one thing for the IMF to venture occasionally into longer-term territory as in the case of the Extended Fund Facility, where the revolving nature of the fund as a whole can still be maintained by virtue of the fact that the vast bulk of the disbursements are for relatively short periods. It becomes, however, a totally different matter if a substantial proportion of IMF resources were to be lent on longer-term. This would court the risk, against which the IMF has been repeatedly cautioned, of transforming itself too far in the direction of a development institution. For this reason we regard the Minister's proposal as essentially transitional. Instead we suggest a procedure whereby governments, as distinct from central banks, take the initiative in establishing a mechanism for re-lending the proceeds of off-market diversification on a genuinely longer-term basis. This is the third and crucial step in the series we recommend.

### Long-term Programme Lending

3.34 The opportunity which is within reach of governments as distinct from central banks (and which could be grasped by them almost *pari passu* with off-market reserve diversification negotiations among central banks), consists

1. J. de Koning: *The Right to Existence and to Development* (address to the Independent Commission on International Development Issues, The Hague, 17 May 1980).

simply of implementing what is perhaps the key recommendation of the Brandt Commission, formulated as follows:

> "We have shown how the 1980s will inevitably see massive increases in the deficits and debts of the developing countries. Further studies are badly needed of the range of those debts and deficits by 1985 and of the resources – both private and public – potentially available to meet them. *But it is already apparent that special measures are needed. The industrialised and the oil-exporting countries should reach agreement on their respective additional roles and additional lending capacities, both directly by each and in the form of jointly shared guarantees.* Given the new sense of the interdependence affecting all parties, it is essential that these two groups of countries join forces to transform this potential crisis into a new opportunity for cooperation – in the common interest".[1]

The existence of a framework of central bank cooperation, which would have the effect of recycling OPEC surpluses off-market and through official (IMF) channels to developing countries, would also facilitate the negotiation of these 'jointly shared guarantees' between governments, which alone would place this lending on an adequately longer-term footing. These guarantees are considered more fully in Appendix 1.

3.35 Whatever arrangements are worked out should make it possible to meet on a systematic rather than an *ad hoc* basis, and with adequate resources, the kinds of need for financing programmes of structural change which are currently being addressed only partially by a clutch of facilities within the Bretton Woods institutions – the Extended Fund Facility within the IMF, limited programme lending within the World Bank, and most recently the World Bank's structural adjustment loans. The area of finance for which there is inadequate provision relates to longer-term programme lending, extending from periods between the five years to which IMF loans are normally limited (or the maximum number of years which the IMF allows under its highly conditional Extended Fund Facility) to the 25 years that applies to Third Window lending by the World Bank. The private banking system has typically operated within the maximum range of IMF maturities and not beyond, and continued recourse to it has the effect of compounding a country's debt problem.

3.36 It would be possible to give effect to the financing arrangements that we have in mind through existing institutions: the World Bank on the one

---

1. Independent Commission on International Development Issues, op. cit., page 279; emphasis added.

hand and the OPEC Special Fund on the other. This would require a relaxation of the rules under which the World Bank engages in programme lending and would also require a substantial addition to the resources made available to the IDA. Alternatively, the financing arrangements might provide the starting-point for a new institution such as the World Development Fund proposed by the Brandt Commission.

3.37 If the Brandt Commission's recommendations were adopted, the 'jointly shared guarantees' that are envisaged as a transitional measure could in due course be given permanent institutional form by their conversion into the callable, as distinct from the paid-in, capital of a lending institution. Callable capital in this sense need represent nothing more than a system of 'limited joint and several guarantees'[1] furnished by the member governments participating in the institution against which the institution is enabled to borrow in the capital markets. An appropriate sequence to implement this third step might then be (a) for the guarantee arrangements alone to be set up among interested countries in the first instance to enable the raising of monies for longer-term programme lending, including in this the proceeds of off-market reserve diversification arrangements which will have been channelled initially through the IMF; and (b) for the determination at a later stage of the paid-in capital obligations that would be required to establish a new institution.

3.38 We are conscious of the difficulties that are likely to arise in worldwide negotiations to implement these two stages. At the same time, some willingness appears to have been shown in current proposals for transforming the OPEC Special Fund into a Development Agency to proceed rapidly enough for the transformation to be completed by the beginning of 1981. In the interests of expediting this process still further during 1980 we suggest that the two stages involved should be sequentially implemented by interested parties.

### Towards a World Development Fund

3.39 The proposals for transforming the OPEC Special Fund, with certain modifications which are described in Appendix 1, could serve two purposes. They could provide the basis for arrangements to meet more adequately the immediate financing needs of net oil-importing developing countries in 1980 and they could also lead to the establishment of the Brandt Commission's World Development Fund. This would involve, in the first place, enabling the OPEC Special Fund to raise, on the basis of supporting guarantees from

1. See Appendix 1.

OPEC governments, up to $8 billion to be disbursed during 1980 to developing countries, on average on Third Window terms. The terms could vary with the circumstances of the borrowing country, so that there was a spectrum of interest rates and maturities ranging from IDA to World Bank terms. The $2 billion available as the undisbursed portion of the $2.4 billion replenishment of the Fund this year would suffice to provide the subsidy element. If OPEC were willing to provide guarantees for up to $8 billion, similar action might also be urged on the developed countries to raise a matching total, with a matching subsidy element, also on the basis of guarantees, in the spirit of the formula for 'jointly shared guarantees' which was proposed by the Brandt Commission. One way in which the developed countries could provide the subsidy element relatively easily, if they were willing to swallow their objections to the principle involved, would be to apply their share of the current round of SDR allocations for this purpose.

3.40 The amount which could eventually be raised in this fashion would be very large – figures of up to $20 billion have been proposed for the OPEC Development Agency alone – and it would be reasonable to expect that a fund or funds of this magnitude, involving developed countries as well, would be in a position to widen its range of activities as compared, for example, with the transformed OPEC Special Fund. While the main area of activity of the fund or funds would always be the provision of long-term programme finance, particularly in the initial years of operation, more resources could over time be devoted progressively to project lending in priority areas such as food and energy and to promoting regional cooperation and integration among developing countries. It would be for consideration whether these activities should be administered by a common agency and the sums raised under two sets of guarantees should be pooled or whether it would be preferable to retain two separate agencies working in close collaboration. The developed countries might prefer to make use of the World Bank rather than set up a new institution and OPEC might be reluctant to entrust large sums to an agency over which its control had to be shared with other countries. In either case, the guarantees could be converted into the callable capital of an agency and the formal institutional arrangements completed by adding in a paid-in capital provision.

3.41 Looked at from the point of view of OPEC, a scheme of this kind might seem a somewhat involved way of making concessionary loans to developing countries, especially as most of the funds borrowed against guarantees would originate with OPEC depositors. They might prefer to use the OPEC Special Fund to make grants or loans on concessionary terms to the countries most in need of immediate help or to give partial relief to those countries. In extreme cases they might even be willing to do both. Given the relatively small quantities of oil involved, the effect of such rebates on oil markets would, with appropriate safeguards, be relatively insignificant. But if either of the possibilities just outlined – grants and soft loans or oil rebates – were adopted to the exclusion of guarantee arrangements, this would be likely to mean sacrificing the more ambitious scheme for a Development Fund in support of loans to accelerate structural change. It would also diminish the likelihood of arrangements, in which the OPEC countries might see virtue, that allowed for participation on equal terms by the developed countries. These are important advantages that it would be a pity to lose. Whatever is done by OPEC, there is an opportunity and a very real need for an initiative by the developed countries in the mutual interest of both developed and developing countries.

# 4. Protectionism and Structural Adjustment

4.1 One of the most damaging consequences of the slowdown of economic growth in the North during the 1970s has been an inward-looking, defensive reaction epitomised by the 'new protectionism'. In the main this takes the form of quantitative restrictions, but it also includes countervailing and anti-dumping action, minimum prices for imports and government aids to ailing industries. Most of these are adopted outside the normal GATT rules and in a discriminatory manner.

### The Spread of Protection

4.2 The new protectionism has been applied so far to a limited number of products. These include textiles and garments, footwear, consumer electronics, motor cars, steel and shipbuilding. But recent developments point dangerously to its widening and intensification, thus confirming its expansive and cumulative nature. Similarly, the proportion of international trade affected by the new protectionism so far is relatively small. But since it is directed largely against labour-intensive imports, some of the affected products make up a substantial proportion of the exports of developing countries. Textiles and garments, the most seriously affected category of manufactures, comprise more than a third of the exports of developing countries to the industrialised countries. A recent estimate for South Korea showed that in 1979 nearly 50 per cent of its exports to the industrialised countries suffered from restrictions of one kind or another. This was almost double the proportion affected in 1975.

4.3 Quantitative restraints are imposed under 'Orderly Marketing Arrangements' (OMAs) and 'Voluntary Export Restraints' (VERs). The former comprise formal agreements laying down targets for the growth rates of imports into the restricting country and of supplies from participating exporters. The latter involve informal agreements in which exporters agree to limit their exports to specified levels.

4.4 The Multi-Fibre Arrangement (MFA) is the most important example of an OMA. Though completely against the spirit of the GATT, it sets the dangerous precedent of being negotiated and administered within the framework of the GATT. It illustrates some of the pernicious effects of protectionism on development prospects. The MFA had its origin in the Long-Term Arrangement on Cotton Textiles established in 1962 and directed at controlling exports mainly from Japan. It was intended to be temporary, to deal with what was described as a unique situation requiring a unique solution. In no way was it to be seen as establishing a precedent. However, in its evolution the arrangement has become entrenched, more comprehensive and increasingly restrictive. Transformed into the Multi-Fibre Arrangement from 1974, it extended its coverage from items of cotton to items of wool and man-made fibres. In 1977 when the MFA was renegotiated, although its text remained unchanged, the GATT waiver under which it operated provided for "reasonable departures". This made it possible for some bilateral agreements to be negotiated which have been more restrictive than the 6 per cent growth of imports allowed under the MFA. The consequence is that the overall growth of exports of the restricted items of textile and clothing from developing countries to the industrialised countries has now fallen significantly. The present MFA comes to an end in 1981. Already there are demands from textile and clothing organisations in the EEC for a more restrictive agreement still. The MFA has also been seen as a possible model for other products such as steel. There is a forceful lobby who advocate the extension of OMAs. They see 'organised free trade' as a central part of international trade policy.

4.5 It cannot be too strongly emphasised that the whole process of economic development is being severely affected by restricted market access. Products such as textiles, clothing and footwear are first-stage manufacturing products for developing countries. When the early growth of exports of manufactured goods is inhibited in this way, economic change is made much more difficult for many developing countries.

### Threat to North and South

4.6 The new protectionism is a threat to the structural changes in world production and trade which are necessary for continuing growth and development. While the proliferation of protective devices has had its most immediate damaging effects on the so-called Newly Industrialising Countries (NICs), it is important to all developing countries. It threatens the prospects of the next generation of industrialising countries – and in the longer-run almost all of the smaller developing countries must seek foreign markets for their manufactures and some of the largest will find it advantageous to do so – but in addition, by slowing down the growth of income and structural change in the NICs, it adversely affects market prospects and development throughout the Third World.

4.7 In the most advanced NICs, such as Korea, Taiwan, Hong Kong and Singapore, rapidly rising real wages have been the fruit of success but also the impetus to further change in comparative advantage whereby these countries move on to the production, for export, of more capital- and technology-intensive products and vacate markets for labour-intensive products to the next generation. Moreover, the rate of growth of industrial production in current and prospective NICs will in considerable measure determine their demand for the primary products, raw materials and foodstuffs, which will remain the staple exports of much of the rest of the Third World. For these reasons, all the Third World shares, in varying degree, the concern of the NICs about the new protectionism and their interest in easier market access through trade liberalisation.

4.8 The paradoxical fact, widely recognised by economists but hard to get across to politicians and the general public, is that resurgent protectionism, while a conspicuous example of policies of the North which hurt the South, does quite as much harm to the economic health of the North itself. Beggar-my-neighbour policies – and much of the resort to higher protection by OECD countries in recent years has been against one another – are liable to spread recession. At the same time, restrictions on imports, whether through tariffs or quantitative controls or other measures to protect high-cost producers, by raising domestic prices add to the forces of cost-price inflation.

4.9 Protectionism has been exacerbated, and rationalised, by the belief that unemployment rates in developed countries are highly sensitive to competition from developing countries. Recent studies do not confirm this view. They have shown that labour displacement brought about by imports from developing countries has generally been negligible. Manufacturing trade between industrialised countries and developing countries has, on the contrary, tended to have a positive effect on employment in the industrialised countries. It is true that industries affected by competition from developing countries tend to be more labour-intensive than export industries, but the overall balance in manufacturing trade between the industrialised and the developing countries is so overwhelmingly in favour of the former that restraints on this two-way trade are likely on balance to have adverse, not beneficial, effects on employment in the industrial countries. Even in terms of gross labour displacement, the effect of competition of imports from developing countries is insignificant compared with other causes of labour displacement, such as technological change, import penetration from other developed countries and demand changes.

4.10 A recent study of this issue with reference to the West German economy has shown that, in the period between 1962 and 1975, 50 times more jobs were lost through growth in labour productivity than through the growth in imports from developing countries.[1] It is pertinent to note also that in the developed countries as a group, 5 million jobs were lost in 1975 through faltering demand. According to another study, relating to the UK economy,[2] the increase in imports of manufactures from 23 NICs during 1970-1975 is estimated to have displaced at most 2 per cent of the 1970 labour force; when account is taken of the effect of increased exports of manufactures to these countries, net displacement was probably zero. These estimates, moreover, make no allowance for positive gains that would have accrued from the higher level of skills in the jobs created than in the jobs lost.

4.11 A survey sponsored by US retail organisations in 1978 found that goods imported from Asia and Latin America were on average sold at retail in the United States for 16 per cent less than domestic products of the same quality. It has been estimated in a recent study that the effects of protectionist measures imposed by the United States between 1975 and 1977 resulted in extra costs to consumers of $660 million for sugar, $1,250 million for carbon steel, $400-$800 million for meat, $500 million for television sets and $1,200 million for footwear.

4.12 It is worth noting also the small extent of import penetration which has actually taken place. Exports of manufactures from developing countries were only 7 per cent of world exports in 1976 and were responsible for less than 2 per cent of the consumption of manufactures by industrialised countries. Even in clothing and textiles, where import penetration was highest, developing countries in 1975 supplied only 8.2 per cent and 3.2 per cent respectively of the consumption of the industrialised countries.

4.13 These facts pose an obvious question: why is there so much protectionism when it can be shown to have such boomerang effects? An important

1. Frank Wolter: *Adjusting to Imports from Developing Countries: The Evidence from a Human Capital-Rich Resource-Poor Country*, in Herbert Giersch (editor): *Reshaping the World Economic Order, Symposium 1976* (Tubingen, 1977).

2. UK Foreign and Commonwealth Office: *The Newly Industrialising Countries and the Adjustment Problem, Report by a Working Group* (London, January 1979).

factor seems to be that while the benefits from foreign competition are diffused and not easy to identify immediately, the social costs are easily identifiable in actual jobs lost and firms which have to diversify to new products, to contract or to close down. This causes an asymmetry in political pressures. What is needed is more information and knowledge about the wider effects of protectionism. This is a task for governments and affected groups such as consumers. It must be carried out if governments are not to continue to be led to adopt irrational and inefficient policies.

4.14 Trade restricting policies not only hamper growth in obvious ways by limiting actual and potential productivity gains and probably have on balance adverse effects on employment but, more fundamentally, they also contribute to what has recently been described as the 'core of the malaise' in the North, 'lost dynamism'. "What make many of these systems now sound like muted versions of 1930s-style secular stagnation are sluggish innovation, dampened investment, lock-ins of resources to low-return uses, impaired reallocation, attenuated competition and fractured markets -- in short, weakened propensities for what OECD has taken to calling 'positive adjustment'."[1]

4.15 Such a diagnosis leads to the conclusion that the relation between faster growth and freer North-South trade is two-way. The correlative of "the standard observation of most diagnoses of protectionist pressures . . . that the best antidote will be accelerated growth and diminished unemployment in the developed countries" is that "by comparison with all realistic alternatives, the combined potency and feasibility of using competition of imports from the developing countries to agitate and stimulate supply-side adjustments in the OECD countries is formidable". "We have a chicken-and-egg phenomenon: trade needs growth but also . . . growth needs trade".[2]

**Positive Adjustment Policies**

4.16 We strongly support this emphasis on "the centrality of trade in a mutual interest agenda".[3] Primary responsibility here lies with the North, and the most general recipe for improvement is well defined by the notion of 'positive adjustment'. We cannot do better than quote a recent statement of its general policy implications:

(i) "Action should be temporary and should, wherever possible, be

---

1. OECD: *Development Cooperation, 1979 Review* (Paris), page 31.

2. Ibid., page 32.

3. Ibid., page 32.

reduced progressively according to a pre-arranged timetable.

(ii) Such action should be integrally linked to the implementation of plans to phase-out obsolete capacity and re-establish financially viable entities, without, however, seeking to raise prices above levels providing an adequate return to efficient producers.

(iii) The cost should be made as evident as possible to decision-makers and the public at large. Careful attention should be paid to the cost to consumers of action which raises prices, to the cost to taxpayers, and to the effects of subsidised competition on employment elsewhere.

(iv) Where public funds are being injected into the private sector, it is desirable that private risk capital should be involved.

(v) Assistance given on a company-by-company basis should be framed so as to provide an incentive for improved management practices, notably by ensuring sufficient domestic and international competition.

(vi) Where the primary objective is to support employment in particular regions or towns, consideration should be given to action that can benefit any eligible company in the area concerned, rather than only those in financial difficulty.

(vii) While recognising that governments must pay due regard to the interests of national security, care should be taken to see that arguments based on considerations of self-sufficiency should not be misused to justify measures for protection and support".[1]

In this spirit, and with the need for freer market access for the developing countries particularly in mind, we list some of the policy initiatives which in our view should have a major place in the North-South dialogue in the months and years to come.

**Maintaining the Momentum of Trade Liberalisation**

4.17 The first need is for the industrialised countries to persevere in the process of trade liberalisation through multilateral trade negotiations (MTNs) along the road travelled by the Kennedy and Tokyo Rounds, and for the developing countries to maintain their political pressure on the industrialised countries for freer access to their markets for Third World manufactures.

---

1. OECD: *The Case for Positive Adjustment Policies* (Paris, June 1979) pages 4-5.

Beyond this, the developing countries should take the maximum advantage of the openings for liberalisation presented by the Tokyo Round. They can do so by signing the Tokyo agreements and thus securing the right to participate actively in the future management of the new codes and in the material benefits which can be achieved under the improved rules of the codes.

**Safeguard Measures**

4.18 One of the most serious obstacles to the liberalisation of trade is abuse by the industrialised countries of 'safeguard measures'. The case for such safeguards to obviate severe disruption of a local industry cannot be rejected entirely, yet once conceded it opens the way wide for restrictive policies. Failure to reach agreement on this issue was a major shortcoming of the Tokyo Round. Discipline in the application of safeguards would have provided some deterrent to protectionist policies. In the event, a GATT Committee of all MTN participants was established to continue negotiations beyond the conclusion of the Tokyo Round. Its aim is to elaborate supplementary rules and procedures regarding the application of Article XIX, so as to provide greater uniformity and certainty in the implementation of its provisions. The Committee was expected to submit a report to the Contracting Parties by 30 June 1980, but at this stage there is no indication of progress on outstanding issues. It is our hope that the negotiations will consider safeguard actions taken not only under Article XIX, but also under other GATT provisions, as well as VERs and OMAs negotiated outside the GATT.

4.19 What is needed is a safeguard system comprehensive in scope and sufficiently flexible in operation to encompass circumstances which, while not a feature of the trading world at the inception of the GATT, are today more the rule than the exception. We strongly support the recommendation of the Brandt Commission that safeguard action should be permitted only under limited and clearly defined conditions; it should be subject to automatic reductions over time and to multilateral control and surveillance, and be linked with the adoption of positive policies of industrial adjustment.

**Barriers to Processing**

4.20 The reduction of tariff escalation on processed products is of concern to many developing countries. Industrialised countries historically have tended to have an initial cost advantage in processing industries for a wide range of raw materials produced in developing countries and have continued to encourage and protect such industries when their cost advantage began to wane. They have done this chiefly by levying higher tariffs on the processed products than on the raw materials. Since such higher tariffs fall largely on the value-added, they provide very high levels of effective protection.

4.21 The Generalised System of Preferences (GSP) was intended to deal with the problem of tariff escalation but it has made little difference. The reduction of tariff escalation on a most favoured nation (mfn) basis thus remains of great importance to developing countries. Even after the Tokyo Round, the degree of tariff escalation for manufactures (CCCN 25-99) is still very marked, as shown by Table 4.1.

4.22 Local processing of raw materials is a form of industrialisation in which developing countries frequently have a comparative cost advantage or the least comparative disadvantage. Its discouragement by tariff escalation is therefore particularly damaging to many countries of the Third World, including the least developed. The rise in the cost of energy in the past decade has tended to shift comparative advantage in energy-intensive processing towards countries with adequate sources of energy, including many in the Third World. They should be helped, not hindered, in taking advantage of this opportunity.

4.23 How large the potential scope for industrial development based on processing can be is indicated by several recent studies. A World Bank study on minerals has shown that in 1970 developing countries obtained less than one-third of the gross value-added they could have generated had they refined their minerals up to the metal ingot stage before export. A more recent UNCTAD study has estimated that developing countries would have earned in 1975 $27 billion more from ten commodities had they undertaken production only up to the semi-processing stage. This amount would be one and a half times the level of export earnings from these commodities. Such figures do not, of course, prove that local processing would in each and every case be an economic use of resources. But they demonstrate that this is an area where trade liberalisation would make a particularly important contribution to development.

**Agricultural Protectionism**

4.24 Protectionism in agriculture has a long history. Unlike trade in manufactures, trade in most agricultural products benefited little if at all from the movement towards trade liberalisation by and among the industrialised countries during the 1950s and 1960s. Indeed, the European Economic Community remains the most conspicuous example of agricultural protectionism. One symptom of this asymmetry is the failure of GATT to apply to agricultural trade the principles it seeks to maintain for trade in manufactures. The feature of agricultural protectionism which permits, if it does not

**TABLE 4.1**

**Tariff Rates on Processed and Unprocessed Imports into Industrialised Countries (percentages)**

| | | Post-MTN tariff averages | |
|---|---|---|---|
| | | Trade-weighted | Simple |
| Wood, pulp, paper and furniture | Raw materials | 0.2 | 0.7 |
| | Semi-manufactures | 1.9 | 3.7 |
| | Finished mfrs. | 4.2 | 5.1 |
| Textiles and clothing | Raw materials | 0.8 | 2.9 |
| | Semi-manufactures | 11.5 | 9.6 |
| | Finished mfrs. | 16.7 | 11.8 |
| Leather, rubber, footwear and travel goods | Raw materials | 0.0 | 1.0 |
| | Semi-manufactures | 4.4 | 4.5 |
| | Finished mfrs. | 10.2 | 10.2 |
| Base metals | Raw materials | 0.0 | 0.2 |
| | Semi-manufactures | 3.2 | 4.6 |
| | Finished mfrs. | 5.9 | 6.1 |
| Minerals, precious stones and metals | Raw materials | 0.3 | 1.4 |
| | Semi-manufactures | 1.1 | 3.6 |
| | Finished mfrs. | 6.9 | 6.5 |

Source: GATT: *The Tokyo Round of Multilateral Trade Negotiations,* Volume II – Supplementary Report (Geneva, January 1980).

justify, this differential treatment is that it largely takes the form of domestic agricultural price support programmes, rather than tariffs or other overt trade restrictions. But the effect on trade is often much more severe, with tariff equivalents frequently well over 100 per cent. Another facet of agricultural protectionism that has made it so pervasive and obdurate is that it derives support from non-economic motives, such as self-sufficiency in food for reasons of national security or protection of the countryside on environmental grounds, which, sound or specious, are not easily brought into an economic calculus. As in the case of industrial protectionism, the benefits to well-organised producer interests are concentrated while the costs to domestic consumers and taxpayers are diffused, and the damage to more efficient foreign producers is discounted.

4.25 In the case of agricultural protectionism, much of this damage falls on the major non-European temperate-zone food producing OECD countries. But developing countries also suffer. Very little progress has so far been made in rationalising agriculture within the EEC. The Common Agricultural Policy is regressive in its effects, since poor consumers, who spend a higher proportion of their incomes on food, and poorer taxpayers provide income transfers to better-off farmers. It has served to discourage movement of people from the land, despite the fact that in the 1960s there were labour shortages in the industrial and service sectors. Internationally, it entails a misallocation of resources since it discourages production in other countries even though they may have a comparative advantage in the products concerned.

4.26 At present, products such as sugar, beef and rice from developing countries are allowed very restricted access to the EEC. This is the case even under the fairly liberal ACP/EEC Lome Convention. EEC sugar policy provides a good example of how inefficient domestic policies can distort world production and trade. Backed up by high internal prices, the EEC has been able to move over the last five years from self-sufficiency to surplus production of over 3 million tons of sugar. The surplus has been dumped on the world market at a cost to the EEC taxpayer of about £350 million in 1979. Meanwhile, the EEC has remained outside the International Sugar Agreement which in order to stabilise prices has over the last two years been restricting supply to the world market. EEC policy appears even more incongruous when account is taken of the fact that most of the increased consumption of sugar in the world is taking place in the developing countries.

4.27 Present GATT rules, for the reasons just mentioned, are tolerant of barriers to agricultural trade. Certain exemptions allow the imposition of import restrictions on agricultural or fisheries products where this is necessary in the enforcement of such governmental measures as domestic agricultural support programmes. In fact, measures adopted at borders, such as tariffs, quotas, variable levies and export subsidies, are usually geared to such programmes. Their relaxation, therefore, becomes closely tied up with domestic farm income and other policy objectives. One of the most perverse aspects of agricultural policies such as the Common Agricultural Policy of the EEC is that they tend to result in huge surpluses which are then often disposed of on world markets by means of overt or covert export subsidies, to the detriment of third-party exporters, whether in other developed or developing countries.

4.28 Although the position of agriculture in the GATT received greater attention in the Tokyo Round than in previous rounds of MTNs, the results were limited. Even after the Tokyo Round, about one-half of agricultural exports from developing countries to industrialised countries remain dutiable at either mfn or GSP rates. The impact of agricultural protection on the exports of developing countries has been assessed in various studies. The latest of such studies, undertaken for FAO in 1979, estimated that a 50 per cent reduction in the protection on food and feed commodities in OECD countries would bring a $3 billion annual increase in aggregate foreign exchange earnings on exports from 57 of the more populous developing countries. Two-thirds of the overall increase in exports would be accounted for by sugar, beef and wine; non-competing products (coffee, cocoa, tea and bananas) would account for 10 per cent.

4.29 A more determined effort is required to liberalise agricultural trade. Such liberalisation is of interest to many developed countries also, and developing countries should join forces with these countries in demanding freer agricultural trade. The EEC should contribute to more stable world markets by less frequent variation in its import levies and by lowering intervention prices. It should certainly phase-out export subsidies and should consider offering guaranteed shares in its market to low-cost producing countries which crucially depend on exports of particular commodities. In the longer-run, it should be persistent in promoting a smaller and more efficient farming sector though liberalisation and structural adjustment, in much the same way and for basically the same good economic reasons as its members rightly demand of countries with traditional policies of industrial protectionism.

4.30 There is no justification for the continuation of barriers of any description on exports from the developing countries of non-competing products. A commitment should therefore be sought for their complete removal as early as possible and in any case not later than the end of 1981. For other products, where free-access would present too great a disturbance to internal farm support or other policies, assistance to developing countries should be in the form of at least partial relaxation of measures, for example enlargement of quotas, duty-rebates, etc., and the scrupulous observance of developing country interests in implementation of the relevant codes on non-tariff measures that emerged from the Tokyo Round.

### Trade with Centrally Planned Economies

4.31 Although trade between developing countries and the socialist countries of Eastern Europe has been expanding rapidly, it remains a very small proportion of world trade, with considerable scope for expansion. In 1977, only 3.7 per cent of the exports of developing countries went to the USSR and other East European countries. Although not significant producers themselves, the socialist countries constitute a large potential market for tropical products such as coffee, bananas and citrus fruits as the standards of living of these countries rise. Trade with centrally planned economies requires of course special trading and payments arrangements and these are at an early stage of development. While the payment problem should not be underestimated as a constraint, centralised decision-making in the socialist countries provides the opportunity for policy decisions which could quickly expand purchases of products of developing countries. The socialist countries could play a substantial role in expanding trade opportunities for developing countries and it is important for economic development that they should take these responsibilities seriously.

### Trade Among Developing Countries

4.32 The expected lower growth rates of the industrialised countries in the foreseeable future, as well as the rise of protectionism, make it necessary for developing countries to pay special attention to the opportunities for trade expansion among themselves. In 1975 intra-developing country trade was responsible for 23 per cent of the exports of developing countries and 35 per cent of their exports of manufactured goods. Recent years have seen some improvement in the relative importance of intra-developing country trade, especially trade in manufactures. The rapid expansion of imports by OPEC has no doubt been a major factor. This points to the great potential for the future. Between 1973 and 1978, exports of manufactures by the non-OPEC developing countries increased at an average annual rate of 22 per cent to industrialised countries, of 35 per cent to OPEC, of 23 per cent to non-OPEC developing countries and of 10 per cent to the Eastern trading area.

4.33 A significant constraint on this trade is the undeveloped state of the infrastructure – shipping linkages, export credit financing and payments arrangements. These must be given priority attention. Trade policy must also be geared to facilitating such trade. There is scope for mutual trade preference schemes, both regional and inter-regional. Some such regional schemes are in existence. The path to greater trade and economic integration has not in all cases been smooth because of the complexities introduced by unequal levels of development and the unequal sharing of benefits and costs. Strains have also been caused by the serious balance of payments problems faced by some member countries in recent years. Such problems should be regarded as challenges, and the opportunities provided for economic development through trade creation from scale and infant industry considerations, especially for smaller countries, must continue to be grasped. Regional and other economic integration schemes among developing countries, however, must be sufficiently outward-looking that the greater trade opportunities with industrialised countries will not be neglected.

**Need for New Initiatives**

4.34 There are clear opportunities for new initiatives. As a consequence of the Tokyo Round, the 35th Session of the GATT Contracting Parties held in November 1979 gave permanent legal sanction to special and differential treatment for developing countries. This now makes possible, for the first time, special MTNs for the express purpose of trade liberalisation by developed countries in favour of developing countries. At such meetings any agreements would be subject to the traditional GATT binding (unlike the GSP). This advantage secured by developing countries should be fully utilised.

4.35 This development comes at the same time as the end of the first ten years of the EEC GSP which, after the modest Australian scheme, was the first to be implemented. The EEC is now giving consideration to the need for basic changes in its scheme. It coincides with the renegotiation of the MFA, which must take place before the end of 1981. The fact that the Tokyo Round did not deal with the relaxation of OMAs and VERs makes this a particularly important issue.

4.36 The time is ripe for a comprehensive examination of the whole problem and for negotiation of access of the exports of developing countries to the markets of the industrialised countries. The global round of North-South negotiations which is to start in 1981 provides an opportunity. Negotiations, and the framework for such trade negotiations, should be a priority subject for the UN Special Session on Development which is to take place in August-September 1980.

4.37 "The great challenge for the North", to quote the Brandt Commission's Report,

> "therefore is to cope with the difficulties of adjustment so that world trade can expand; to see its trade with the South not as a threat but as an opportunity; to see it not only as part of the problem but as part of the solution. In the end, failure of the mature industrial economies to adjust to the realities of international competitiveness may deprive them of their prosperity and impose far costlier and more disruptive adjustments than those which their current measures of protection attempt to postpone. The industrialised countries cannot expect their valuable exports to developing countries to continue (and the large loans by commercial banks to several of them to be repaid) if they do not permit them to earn their way by selling their manufactures in return. The challenge to the South is to develop the necessary expertise and trained manpower to ensure their own industrial development and to respond positively to the trade opportunities created by improved access to the markets of the North. Considerable mutual interests of North and South lie in the changes in the world economy implied by the South's industrialisation".[1]

---

1. Independent Commission on International Development Issues, op.cit., pages 70-71.

# 5. The Inflation Problem

5.1 In the course of the past decade inflation has come increasingly to dominate the international scene. In the 1950s it remained around 3 per cent in most OECD countries and was only slightly higher in the 1960s. But in the 1970s it increased sharply and is now in double figures in many of the major industrialised countries. Many of the developing countries have also suffered from high and accelerating inflation.

5.2 This acceleration coincided with the increase in oil prices in 1973-74, just as the more recent acceleration of inflation in 1979-80 coincided with a fresh increase in oil prices. But oil was not the primary cause in either case. Rather it followed and reinforced a general price rise that was already in progress. Moreover, although every country had to face the steep rise in oil prices, the rate of inflation did not show an equal response in every country. In Germany and Japan, for example, the acceleration after 1973 was comparatively mild while in the United Kingdom and Italy it was very much greater.

5.3 The movement in commodity prices which was the most prominent symptom of inflation in 1973-74 was caused by a combination of circumstances: a boom in the industrialised countries; the monetary expansion of the early 1970s and the search for alternative assets and the commodity speculation to which this led; the break-up of fixed exchange rates; and an abnormal grouping of harvest failures. It is not necessary to investigate the relative importance of each of these or the manner in which they interacted with one another. It is material, however, that the rise in one set of prices was not offset by a fall in other prices. On the contrary, the efforts of income-earners in the industrialised countries to avoid the reduction in their real incomes implicit in the rise in input prices were reflected in larger wage-claims and in due course in larger wage-settlements, and monetary and fiscal policies tended to respond to those pressures. Added to this, the strain of a higher import-bill on some of the weaker currencies forced down the value of those currencies and magnified the movement in commodity prices when expressed in those currencies. Thus what started as a shift in the terms of trade that had no inescapable consequences for the general level of prices was translated, via currency devaluation, 'real-wage resistance' and permissive monetary policies, into an alarmingly high rate of inflation. On the other hand, those countries that accepted more readily the burden of higher commodity prices or whose currencies were not depreciated suffered less severely from an acceleration in inflation.

5.4 Whatever the causes of the acceleration in inflation it has had harmful effects on growth. Some would emphasise direct effects. Inflation distorts the calculus of economic decision-making by disturbing established price relationships and introducing additional uncertainty. It becomes much harder to assess the return on new investment and to plan for the future with confidence. Inflation also plays on the fears of those who are hit by it and creates resentments towards those who benefit.

5.5 Others would regard the indirect effects of rapid inflation on economic activity and growth as more important. These come about through the changes in the attitude and policy of governments as inflation takes hold. Governments become increasingly willing to acquiesce in a slowing down of growth as a means of keeping it under control. They are alarmed both by the acceleration that has occurred and by the spread of inflationary expectations. The first of these makes the control of inflation more urgent amd the second makes it more difficult. The more inflation is taken for granted the harder it is to shake it off or keep it within limits. Interest rates rise to reflect the expected change in the value of money and borrowers acquire a vested interest in a rate of inflation that depreciates their debt obligations on the scale expected. Similarly wage-earners enter claims based on their experience of inflation in the recent past and so perpetuate past rates. With budgets already in deficit, partly because of the depressed level of economic activity, governments are reluctant to sanction increased government spending or carry tax reductions much beyond offsetting cuts in expenditure.

5.6 Domestic demand management policies can have serious repercussions on other countries. For example, when the United States in 1929 pushed up interest rates it did so in order to get on top of a speculative boom, but in the process it attracted funds from all over the world and forced deflationary policies on other countries at just the wrong moment. The same thing could happen again if large countries use monetary restraint to check inflation without regard to the resulting capital flows and their effects in forcing weaker countries to contract credit in difficult circumstances. Conversely, excessively expansionary policies in the United States are widely believed to have been a major factor behind the acceleration of inflation throughout the world economy in the years 1970-1972 and again in 1977-1979.

5.7 The relative emphasis placed on the direct and indirect effects of inflation on growth and on the dangers to other countries of excessively lax or excessively stringent demand management is at the heart of the current controversies between two schools of thought. The monetarist school attaches importance to the growth of money supply as a causal or at least a permissive factor in inflation, and to monetary restraint as an essential remedy. Their opponents attribute inflation mainly to excessive income claims and believe that monetary restraint cannot by itself make enough impact on inflation to justify its adverse effects on economic activity and employment.

5.8 On the one hand, are those economists who would favour operating on the money supply as a means of resisting inflationary pressure, and on the other hand are those who would seek to operate directly on costs and particularly on wage-settlements. From this point of view it hardly matters whether the monetary or the fiscal ingredient in demand management is uppermost in the minds of policy-makers. If inflation can be controlled by operating on demand, and if the control of inflation takes precedence over other aims of policy, then it is difficult to justify expanding demand under inflationary conditions. On the other hand, if wages go their own way without much regard to the level of demand, then action to restrict demand, monetary or fiscal, will merely depress economic activity without slowing down the rate of inflation.

5.9 The difference in analysis between the opposing views can be illustrated in terms of the macro-economic impact to be expected from a rise in oil prices. Most economists, and particularly those reared on Keynesian ideas, would expect such a rise, or indeed any general rise in import prices, to be passed on to the consumer so that the resulting increase in the cost of living reduced consumer purchasing power. They would then predict that, in the absence of government intervention, there would be a simultaneous fall in profits and job opportunities and a rise in current wage claims to make good the reduction in living standards. Given the attitude and bargaining power of the trade unions, they would expect to see employers yield to these claims, to some degree at least, so that price inflation received a further stimulus. Meanwhile, the government, confronted by rising unemployment, would be likely to acquiesce in the loss of revenue and higher outgoings involved in the lower level of economic activity and consequent unemployment; and it might even seek to offset some of this contraction by additional spending and a still higher budget deficit. If the oil producers were slow to absorb their increased earnings in higher living standards or domestic capital formation, the upshot would be that the industrial world as a whole would end up by borrowing back what was not absorbed and using the oil producers' extra savings to finance budget deficits in the public sector and producers' losses in the private sector of their various economies. The use of extra savings would help to keep up real income and consumption levels above what could be afforded in the longer run. Under these conditions inflation of prices would have failed to achieve its fundamental purpose of choking-off demand in conformity with the adverse movement in the terms of trade. The position would remain one of disequilibrium, reflected on the one side in higher earnings not fully absorbed and on the other in distress borrowing, illusory expectations of undiminished real incomes, and inflation as the expression of the disproportion between illusion and reality.

5.10 A monetarist would take a more radical view of the situation. He would point out that if one price or set of prices goes up, this may require (or cause) other prices to come down if stability in the price level is to be preserved. He would deny that there is some basic or underlying rate of inflation that must be taken for granted and to which fresh inflationary impulses from outside the system can simply be added. To accept such an assertion would amount, as the GATT Report for 1978/79 contends, to "an abdication of government responsibility in the face of inflation".[1] Similarly, if the steeper inflationary trend is then built into wage settlements, this will prove self-defeating if the central bank stands firm and refuses to 'validate' excessive increases in wages by increasing the money supply. No doubt this refusal will bring about higher unemployment; but the alternative of fuelling inflation will in the end do more harm to growth and employment.

5.11 It is also contended by monetarists that a rise in oil prices need exercise no serious and prolonged deflationary influence on economic activity in oil-importing countries. If all that is involved is a change in the terms of trade between oil-exporting and oil-importing countries, the impact on world economic activity should, they argue, be small and transitional. To the objection that severe deflationary forces could be unleashed if the OPEC countries were to accumulate large liquid funds, monetarists would reply that there is indeed a danger of cumulative recession. But it arises from the possible inability or unwillingness of oil-importing countries to finance balance of payments deficits, pending correction of such deficits through structural adjustment. So long as the OPEC countries continue to run current account surpluses, the proceeds must be held, that is to say lent and spent, somewhere.

1. GATT: *International Trade 1978/79* (Geneva, 1979), page 15.

5.12 The difference between the two views largely reflects different judgements about facts which are uncertain, though differences of analysis and 'paradigm' also play a part. We cannot pretend to be able to resolve them. In the context of policy, the underlying issue is at what cost inflation can be halted or at least slowed down. The monetarists emphasise the need for monetary restraint and treat any unemployment arising on the way as a necessary and temporary price. Non-monetarists are reluctant to accept any degree of monetary restraint without regard to the severity of its effect on economic activity and employment. They accept trade union attitudes and other competing claims on resources as a fact of life in western societies and seek remedy in some form of incomes policy, as the only alternative to insupportable contractions of income and employment.

5.13 The correct mix of policies, monetary or non-monetary, can only be decided by governments. There are no universal or agreed solutions and policies are likely to vary from country to country depending partly on political and institutional factors. Whatever may be the best mix of policies from the national point of view, it is appropriate to stress that due account must be taken of the effect of these policies on other countries. Policies conceived in purely domestic terms may be neither appropriate nor effective.

5.14 One point that can be made emphatically is that the control of inflation, whether on a domestic or a world-wide basis, demands more effective management of domestic economies and more concerted effort to regulate the world economy through new international arrangements. In this connection, we would like to underline the following suggestion by the United Nations Committee for Development Planning at its meeting in January 1980:

> "Greater predictability and longer term assurance in the prices and supplies of commodities in the 1980s would also make a useful contribution to a more stable and positive international economic environment. . . . New efforts should be made over the coming years, recognising the need for such agreements to cover greater stability and predictability of real prices as well as greater security of supplies, and to cover a number of major commodities not just oil or energy."[1]

5.15 Inflation, to sum up, poses a serious threat to the prosperity and growth of the world economy. It represents a failure of economic management that will be costly to remedy and the cost will not fall only on those countries where the failure has been greatest. Each country has to wrestle with the problem in terms of its own local circumstances and priorities. But

---

1. United Nations: *Committee for Development Planning: Report on the Sixteenth Session* (New York, 1980), paragraph 27.

it is to be hoped that in their efforts to put an end to one evil, countries do not lose sight of their obligations to one another or of the even greater evils that might be let loose on the world by too single-minded, over-zealous and wrong-headed remedies.

# 6. The Energy Issue

6.1 Energy was one of the dominant issues of the 1970s. World attention focused primarily on the four-fold increase in the price of oil in 1973-74 and the doubling in 1979,[1] and on the critical limits to petroleum as a major source of energy. The unforeseen, sudden and sharp increases in the price of oil have created major problems for oil-importing countries. Apart from the effect on costs and prices, they have, as we have noted, created balance of payments problems.

6.2 In Chapter 3 we have emphasised the urgent need for initiating appropriate financial arrangements to provide adequate balance of payments support to oil-importing countries. In the longer-run, however, the solution to the energy problem must lie in increasing its availability through an accelerated programme of exploration and development of all forms of energy and by reducing the consumption of energy per unit of GDP through conservation measures. In this chapter we consider the supply and the conservation aspects of the energy issue.

### Investment in Exploration

6.3 Available studies on resource levels of traditional fossil fuels (oil, coal, gas) and of nuclear fuels indicate that though these are of course finite, there are immense reserves that still remain to be proved, let alone exploited. It is widely held that the level of proved reserves of energy has been held down by three main factors. The first is the low price and abundant supplies of Middle East oil until 1973; this militated against any intensive search for other sources of energy, for example coal, or of oil in most importing countries. The second is what many consider to be a misallocation of investment in energy exploration; because of 'political' risks and other influences, too great a proportion of the total investment has been directed away from other

1. By contrast the real price of oil had fallen during the period 1975-78.

promising areas. The third factor is the heightened uncertainty in the energy market and the difficulty in foreseeing the future course of prices of oil and other sources of energy.

6.4 Immediately following the steep oil price increases in 1973, there was a substantial upsurge of investment in the exploration for fossil fuels, particularly oil. But the 1974 level was not fully maintained in subsequent years. Most of the investment took place in the developed countries. This might be considered somewhat surprising since many of the potential oil-bearing sedimentary basins are in the developing countries.[1] It has meant that a higher proportion of the ultimately recoverable oil resources estimated to exist in the developed countries has now been discovered than of those in the non-OPEC developing countries, which remain largely undiscovered. This comparative reluctance to invest in oil exploration in most developing countries also applies to other minerals.[2]

6.5 Doubtless there are several reasons for this. As with other minerals, exploration for oil is risky in a geological sense and these risks are likely to be greater when drilling takes place in an unknown environment, particularly if the technical and other infrastructural facilities are weak. Higher transport costs have increased the attractiveness of producing nearer to the final market. Above all, there seems to be a view that investment in exploration within many developing countries is 'politically' too risky as the terms of the contract may be varied after oil has been discovered. In view of the expense involved, such uncertainty is believed to have a discouraging effect on potential investors. However, the high geological risk and costs involved in oil exploration make it difficult, in many cases impossible, for developing countries themselves to undertake or commission such exploration.

6.6 There is a need, therefore, for a mutual understanding between the investors and the host government regarding a fair sharing of the gains from

---

1. It has been estimated that in 1976, outside the centrally planned economy countries, 64 per cent of the potentially oil-bearing land was to be found among the developing countries but that only 28 per cent of the oil exploration expenditure took place in these countries. See UN: *A programme to accelerate petroleum production in the developing countries* (Economic and Social Council, 30 May 1979); and Kamal Hossain: *Law and policy in petroleum development* (Frances Pinter, London, 1979).

2. According to a submission in 1977 to the President of EEC Commission by fourteen mining companies, exploration by EEC mining companies in developing countries had fallen from 57 per cent of their overall expenditure in 1961 to 13.5 per cent on average during 1973-1975.

exploration and development of oil resources. One way in which exploration contracts can be improved is by adopting a tax formula which incorporates the principle of a 'resource rent tax'. Several variations of this are possible. One is a progressive scheme of production-sharing under which the proportion going to the government would increase in accord with the size of output. Another is a share participation arrangement whereby the amount of equity acquired by the host country would vary according to the profitability of the enterprise. A number of countries have recently made contracts incorporating a 'resource rent tax' principle[1] and several more have them under consideration. We believe the wider adoption of the 'resource rent tax' principle in oil and other mineral concession agreements will make these agreements more stable, and thus reduce some of the non-geological risks which are currently inhibiting exploration for energy (and other minerals) in developing countries.

6.7 More generally, we also wish to emphasise the crucial need to construct agreements in such a way that their provisions give the host government overall control over the venture and a substantial share of the ensuing income and profits (through royalties, taxes and dividends) while at the same time attracting sufficient capital, technology and managerial skills to ensure a high level of exploration expenditure and other prerequisites for the success of the venture. At present, it seems that such agreements would probably be of a hybrid nature incorporating elements of joint venture agreements, production-sharing arrangements and service contracts, with a considerable degree of inbuilt flexibility. Eventually, however, the most appropriate form of contract may be one in which the operating enterprise is paid a sum consisting in part of a return on its capital invested and in part of a fee on the services it provides. Meanwhile, more technical assistance should be made available to developing country governments in order that they may be in a position to negotiate more equitable and therefore more stable contracts with energy transnationals.

6.8 We also see a need for host governments to undertake thorough and comprehensive geological and geophysical surveys and assessments of their countries' energy potential before entering into contracts with the energy transnationals. Although energy exploration is much less expensive than energy development (in the case of oil, for example, the ratio is approximately 1:50), it is still relatively costly (say \$2-\$5 million for an oil project). This is especially so when it is, as for most developing countries, almost entirely a foreign exchange cost. Some developing countries would, there-

---

1. Including the Governments of Papua New Guinea and Tanzania.

fore, find it difficult to finance such operations themselves. In those cases what is required is a mechanism to provide third-party financing. We recognise that such mechanisms already exist and that a certain amount of funding is now available, for example from the World Bank since January 1979. But the size of these funds has been small in relation to the expressed needs (and on present policies is likely to remain so), while the terms and conditions have caused difficulties for the poorer countries.

6.9 Substantially increased funds on easier terms will have to be made available to assist developing countries in energy exploration, particularly for oil. Since it is desirable to avoid the proliferation of institutions, the most appropriate approach may be further expansion of the World Bank's current energy programme. But there is also a case for extension and strengthening of the UN Revolving Fund to include energy minerals and to ease the terms on which repayments are made.

6.10 The funds for an expanded World Bank energy programme and an extended and strengthened UN Revolving Fund would necessarily have to be sought mainly from the developed countries and OPEC. It is obviously in the interest of OECD member countries that energy supplies in oil-importing developing countries should be increased as quickly and as much as possible. This would (a) reduce the potential increase in their import demands from present sources, for example oil from OPEC, and (b) lead to the possibility of new sources of energy becoming available for export, for example oil from Mexico. OPEC members also have an interest in assisting in actions which would (a) take pressure off their own production and thus help to conserve what will become an increasingly scarce non-renewable resource (which is also their main source of wealth), and (b) help fellow Third World countries to accelerate their economic development, especially in heavy industries and other energy-intensive sectors.

6.11 The very much larger sums needed for the energy development stage and the inherently risky nature of many of the processes involved, make it difficult if not impossible for official multilateral facilities to provide a substantial part of the finance required. The bulk of this must continue to come from commercial sources, and the most useful role we see for official multilateral facilities is in providing relatively small amounts of loan capital. In this and other ways, such as ensuring that adequate pre-investment surveys are undertaken, they would act as a catalyst to reassure transnationals and thus encourage them to invest in developing countries.

6.12 Consideration also needs to be given to the even larger financial requirements necessary for adequate development, production, transport and distribution of alternative sources of energy. Apart from oil and natural gas, and as yet unexploited reserves of hydroelectric power, the only alternative sources which are economic on a large-scale with existing technology are coal and nuclear power. Both present serious environmental problems – albeit of a different nature – and further technological work is urgently needed to minimise these hazards. But there is little doubt that most incremental growth in energy consumption in the next twenty or thirty years will have to come from these two sources.

**Development of Energy Potential**

6.13 Larger research resources are also urgently needed for improvement in the efficiency of exploitation and use of conventional fuels and for the development of new sources of energy. We understand that under present operating conditions over half the global energy available in the reserves worked is lost. Energy recovery efficiency (i.e. the relationship between the amount of primary energy produced and that of the energy reserve worked) varies considerably from one source to another.[1] Given the necessary economic incentives, however, the maximum use of presently available technologies could raise the recovery factor substantially. In the case of the ECE region, for example, it has been estimated that between the mid-1970s and the early 1990s, the average recovery factor could technically be raised from 46 per cent to 71 per cent, although the practically attainable level was more likely to be around 59 per cent.[2] The sharpest increase could be realised for the scarcest energy resource – petroleum – where the present average of 35 per cent can be raised to 40-50 per cent with the aid of secondary recovery techniques and to 50-60 per cent with that of tertiary techniques. To maximise the petroleum produced from known resources (including such sources as shale-oil and tar-sands) we see the need for greater incentives to make the best possible use of available recovery techniques: as these are usually expensive, financial assistance might be considered for the poorer of the developing countries which are producing oil for their domestic requirements.

6.14 In addition there is a need to foster R & D into harnessing new sources of energy, such as solar energy (whether directly from the sun or indirectly

---

1. From 80 to 90 per cent for opencast coal mines, 60 to 80 per cent for underground 'longwall' coal mines and dry natural gas wells, to 35 per cent for underground 'room and pillar' coal mines and onshore oil wells.

2. See UN: *Increased Energy Economy and Efficiency in the ECE Region* (Economic Commission for Europe, 1976).

as in the form of wind energy, tidal energy, ocean thermal energy, etc.) and geothermal energy. Research resources are needed both to solve technological problems and to reduce costs of using known technologies. Although these types of renewable energy (unlike hydraulic resources and biomass) cannot be expected to make a significant contribution to world energy supplies before the end of the century, it is essential for assuring the long-term supply of energy that adequate resources are put into R & D in this field. For the same reason, and looking further into the future, research into fusion power should be continued by those nations in a position to undertake it.

6.15 Meanwhile, developing countries are facing a number of vital constraints when they attempt to provide from their own resources the large-scale, often specialised and complex, technologies required for energy supply systems. The chief of these constraints is a deficiency in skilled manpower, particularly of engineering and managerial personnel. From that follow other constraints, for example inadequate information on technologies available and knowledge about the prospects of their future development, a lack of expertise in negotiating for them, an insufficient ability to absorb or adapt received technologies or to develop new ones, and an inadequate capacity to manufacture or in some cases even to service, energy plant and equipment. Technical assistance is required to help those countries overcome these problems.

6.16 We are aware that a significant amount of assistance in the energy field is available from the UN and other multilateral sources, as well as from bilateral sources. Yet there is abundant evidence of need for expanded assistance programmes and for more facilities. We have noted that various proposals have been made to overcome the gaps which exist, but little action appears to have resulted. We can but echo the call of others for the international community to take early measures to assist developing countries to establish or strengthen their energy technology training facilities and R & D institutions.

**Energy Conservation**

6.17 Energy conservation is a term open to varying interpretations. We have used it to embrace all efforts directed toward reducing the amount of energy consumed per unit of GDP generated. Reducing the energy-intensity of economic growth may be achieved in several ways, including (a) restructuring final demand, (b) changing consumers' energy-using practices, and (c) applying improved technologies for energy production, transport, conversion and utilisation. In a dynamic world these changes are likely to take place simultaneously in response to the effects of supply/demand factors and/or government policies on price and other means of influencing or determining consumption.

6.18 There are well-known secular and cyclical factors affecting the energy-intensiveness of the economy. On the one hand, countries tend to become more energy-intensive as their economies industrialise, their societies urbanise and the proportion of energy used in secondary or converted form (such as thermal electricity) rises. The newly industrialising of the developing countries are perhaps the best current example of this stage. On the other hand, there is some evidence that countries tend to become less energy-intensive as their economies mature further and the services and other tertiary sectors grow in relative importance. Superimposed on these secular trends is a continuing movement toward lessening energy-intensity which accompanies the general technological progress upon which much economic growth is based.

6.19 Around these secular trends there are cyclical movements which, by affecting the more energy-intensive sectors of the economy (for example steel, aluminium, cement, chemicals and other branches of heavy industry) to a greater degree than the less energy-intensive ones (for example services), can lead to marked changes in the relationship of total energy consumed to that of aggregate GDP generated. Although higher prices for energy have had a significant effect on fuel consumption, cyclical movements in the composition of GDP have probably so far made a larger contribution than higher consumer prices and other energy conservation measures to the remarkable drop in the energy/GDP coefficients registered by OECD countries since 1974.[1] If there is a return during the 1980s to significantly higher economic growth in OECD, these exceptionally low coefficients are not expected to be maintained.[2] This is mainly because such a return presupposes recovery and growth in production by the energy-intensive sectors.

6.20 Whilst it is widely recognised that the relocation of certain economic

1. The OECD countries' aggregate energy/GDP coefficient (i.e. the average percentage change in their energy consumption divided by the average percentage change in their GDP) averaged 0.9 during 1970-73, when the average annual growth rate of GDP was 4.7 per cent, but only 0.3 during 1974-78, when GDP average annual growth was reduced to 2.7 per cent.

2. Forecasts by the Secretariat of the International Energy Agency for its member countries (which comprise 21 of the 24 OECD countries) are for energy/GDP coefficients averaging 0.84 during 1978-85 and 0.81 during 1985-90, on assumed GDP annual growth rates averaging 4.2 per cent and 3.6 per cent respectively.

activities between countries is a continuing and, indeed, in a dynamic global economy an inevitable process, it is equally one which in general takes a comparatively long time to have significant effects. A rising real price of energy may alter the present optimum location of economic activities, particularly those in the manufacturing sector, in so far as it raises the transport component of costs, especially in the case of coal. For that reason it is possible, and perhaps likely, that a greater part than hitherto of the new production capacity coming into operation in the more energy-intensive sectors during the next twenty years or so will be located in those countries which possess abundant domestic supplies of energy. But this is not to say that we necessarily foresee a substantial and swift relocation of currently installed capacity. Moreover, to the extent that a restructuring of final demand for energy does take place in individual countries through a relocation of certain of their economic activities, this would be of potential assistance to energy conservation only within those countries, although it would help improve global use of a scarce resource. Measures to economise in the use of energy for particular purposes must therefore be continued, particularly (but not exclusively) in the energy-deficit countries. One way in which this can be achieved is through changing consumers' energy-using practices by greater employment of the price mechanism and other regulatory forces.

6.21 We are aware of the various measures taken by member countries of the International Energy Agency (IEA) since 1974 to change consumers' energy-using practices and have noted the conclusions of the IEA Secretariat that those measures which have contributed most significantly to that end were appropriate pricing policies, financial and fiscal incentive schemes, regulations on energy-efficiency standards, and public information and advice programmes. We have also noted the IEA Secretariat's conclusion that those member countries which had experienced the largest increases in energy prices and in other respects had the strongest conservation programmes had been those in which the amount of energy consumed per unit of GDP had diminished most, and that the strength and comprehensiveness, and therefore the effectiveness, of the various national programmes had differed considerably.

6.22 We believe particular attention should be paid by governments to implementing a more appropriate pricing policy for the consumption of energy, especially of petroleum products, and that those countries, such as the United States, in which prices are currently restrained by domestic controls should take early action to effect decontrol (or where that is already scheduled, to accelerate the process). Prices of all energy products paid by domestic consumers should at the very least reflect the world market price of supplies of the marginal fuel (at present oil) and the cost of transporting, converting and distributing those products to the user. Such a pricing policy is essential for a better allocation of scarce energy resources. An active fiscal policy (for example the imposition of excise duties) may well be necessary to achieve that end. These conclusions are applicable to all countries, including oil-exporting countries. In the case of certain items of importance to the poor in developing countries, such as domestic grades of kerosene (vital for cooking and lighting), a transitional period of adjustment may well be necessary, although this should be kept as short as possible.

6.23 A second major area of conservation policies is setting and enforcing regulations on energy-efficiency standards. These are particularly important in the transport sector. We suggest mandatory fuel economy standards, of the type operated in the United States,[1] should be adopted immediately by other countries and made progressively more stringent in their application. Standards also have a valuable role to play in the residential sector. We consider they should be a mandatory part of the building regulations and also be applied to all domestic electrical appliances.

6.24 Lastly, there are the public information and advice programmes on energy conservation. These are especially significant in the industrial sector, where the technical possibilities are more complex than elsewhere. Particular emphasis should be given to such aspects as optimising patterns of fuel utilisation (for example the replacement of oil by other sources of energy).

6.25 As a means of enforcing energy conservation, we also see considerable merit in indirect actions such as the oil-import targets adopted by IEA member countries since October 1977 and made more stringent by the monitoring provisions and national allocation procedures agreed at their December 1979 Ministerial Meeting. Such arrangements should be continued and consideration given to extending them to major oil-importers among the developing countries[2] as part of a global energy policy to which we draw attention in the concluding section of this chapter (see paragraph 6.36).

6.26 Given that fossil fuels are a depletable and increasingly scarce resource, each of the above measures is applicable to all countries, whether developed or developing, energy-surplus or energy-deficit. In practice, the mere fact that

---

1. These include mandatory fuel-efficiency standards for passenger cars manufactured after 1977, progressive taxation of car manufacturers if their models fail to reach specified mileage standards, and mandatory speed limits.

2. For example, Brazil, Korea, Turkey, Taiwan, India, Philippines, Thailand, Cuba, Singapore.

the developed market economy countries account for over half of the world's consumption of commercial energy and for almost two-thirds of its oil means that, *prima facie,* the scope for energy conservation should be much greater in those countries than in the developing countries, where civilian, or at any rate household, consumption is generally small and in most cases used for purposes vital to their industrial or agricultural production and distribution. Yet if the prospects of energy conservation in the developing countries through a lessening of the energy-intensiveness of their economies, or of an elimination of inessential use, are comparatively poor, the relatively inefficient use made of much of the energy consumed means that the scope for conservation through technical improvements is very much greater. It is to this aspect that we now turn.

6.27 Although the efficiency of energy technologies has been improving for generations, scope for further advance by applying known techniques and developing new ones is still vast. We have already drawn attention to the scope for increasing the efficiency of energy recovery at the primary production stage (paragraph 6.13); opportunities are even greater further along the chain. Although the relative efficiency of use of energy varies significantly from one country to another, depending on such variables as the proportion of primary energy converted into secondary forms before use (for example thermal electricity), estimates suggest that in most industrialised countries over a quarter of the primary energy produced is lost in conversion into secondary energy and in distribution, while a further two-fifths is lost in transforming the delivered energy into useful energy. Overall, it appears that around five-sixths of the caloric content of exploited deposits of primary sources of energy is lost on its way into final use: around one-sixth of this loss occurs at the extraction stage and four-sixths at the transport, conversion, distribution and utilisation stages.[1]

6.28 In absolute amounts, the biggest single loss in the industrialised countries has been in energy conversion and distribution. The main reason is the widespread and increasing conversion of primary energy into electricity, where the average net thermal efficiency of generating stations is currently only about 32 to 35 per cent. On a proportionate basis, however, the greatest loss has occurred in the transport sector, where around 80 per cent of the delivered energy is lost in transformation into useful energy. By comparison the loss in the industrial sector has been estimated to be a little under half and that in the residential and services (commercial and public administration) sector at rather over half.

1. For further details see, for example, UN (ECE), op. cit. and Fred Roberts: *The scope for energy conservation in the EEC* (Energy Policy, June 1979).

6.29 We do not propose to list here the many technical possibilities which might lead to savings of energy, both within the energy industry itself and in other sectors of the economy. These have been the subject of extensive study elsewhere[1] and in any case their applicability varies according to individual circumstances, such as comparative fuel costs. Increasing public awareness of the progress of energy technologies, and the ability to acquire, absorb and supply them, will demand not only greater efforts by national governments but also increased international cooperation of the type we have mentioned earlier (paragraph 6.16).

6.30 Estimates of the expected size of energy savings per unit of GDP achieved by restructuring final demand, changing consumers' energy-using practices and applying known energy technologies vary from source to source and from one time horizon to another. A study[2] undertaken for the Conservation Commission of the World Energy Conference, for example, estimated that by 2020 global savings in the ratio of energy demand to gross world product might be 46 per cent compared with 1975: 29 per cent of this would be derived from improved technological efficiency and the remainder from structural changes in energy use (including conservation policies) and in the world economy. Shorter-term estimates, by other sources, suggested savings of one-third for the ECE region between the mid-1970s and the early 1990s[3], and 10-15 per cent for IEA countries between 1975 and 1985 if they were to follow vigorous and systematic energy conservation policies.[4] Studies of particular countries have often come to quite startling conclu sions. One has demonstrated in great detail how the United Kingdom could increase its GDP two- or three-fold between 1976 and 2025 and at the same time consume 22 per cent and 8 per cent respectively less primary energy in 2025 than in 1976. In doing so it would still be making use only of currently known and demonstrated technologies.[5] Another has concluded that "with sufficiently high energy prices over the next few decades, the

1. See, for example, the proceedings of the World Energy Conferences (especially the *Report of the Conservation Commission of the Tenth World Energy Conference* held in September 1977) and Gerald Leach et al: *A Low Energy Strategy for the United Kingdom* (IIED Science Reviews, 1979).

2. L.Nevanlinna and F. Kommonen: *Report on Energy Conservation for the Conservation Commission of the World Energy Conference,* 1979.

3. UN (ECE), op. cit.

4. Statement by Ulf Lantzke, Executive Director of IEA, to *OECD Economic Observer,* November 1979.

5. Gerald Leach et al., op. cit.

United States could double the efficiency with which is uses energy without significant adverse effect on economic growth".[1]

6.31 We have not been able to assess the validity of these statements. We are, however, aware that their fulfilment will depend in large measure on the vigour with which governments apply conservation policies, facilitate and promote the transfer, assimilation and application of existing technologies to raise energy efficiencies and stimulate the development of new technologies. Greater international cooperation as well as national resolve will be needed to achieve that end.

**Need for a Global Energy Policy**

6.32 Given the level of energy resources, and assuming the investment of adequate resources into energy exploration and development as well as into R & D for new technologies, the actual amount of energy supplied will still depend ultimately on the production policies followed. The long gestation period between the start of energy exploration and that of production, transport and distribution, which is often of the order of a decade or more, means that, in broad terms, the upper limit of global energy production during most of the 1980s has already been set by past decisions on exploration and development.

6.33 But the uncertainties engendered by the change in institutional framework of the major oil-exporting countries during the late 1960s and first half of the 1970s, and by the divergent perceptions of different interest groups (including environmentalists and conservationists), meant that the expansion of investment in the world energy industry which should have been generated by the 1973-74 oil price rises did not occur to the extent needed to diversify and extend sufficiently the global energy base. The market economy countries remained too dependent on Middle East oil, while most centrally planned economy countries became increasingly reliant on Soviet oil. At the start of the 1980s several major oil-exporting countries cut production,[2] whilst it was known that Saudi Arabian output was at a rate significantly above its desired ceiling. Many commentators see OPEC oil production rising only slowly during the 1980s and perhaps not at all during the second half of the decade. Other, more pessimistic, projections indicate that its

1. United States National Academy of Sciences: *Energy in transition, 1985-2010* (US Department of Energy, Washington, January 1980).

2. Examples include Libya, Kuwait, Iraq, Iran, Venezuela.

production will never again exceed the 1979 level.[1]

6.34 The reasons for what some see as a fundamental change in OPEC production policies are diverse and complex. There are economic factors, such as the reluctance to exchange an appreciating asset (oil in the ground) for a depreciating or frozen one (dollar deposits and investments abroad) and the desire of some governments to preserve as much as possible of their oil-wealth for the benefit of future generations. There are also complex social and political factors which tend to reinforce these economic considerations.

6.35 On the economic side we see an urgent need to devise a mechanism to protect oil-exporters' revenues invested in the West. We have proposed such a mechanism in Chapter 3 and suggest urgent attention be given to this and other possible mechanisms. Otherwise it is possible that OPEC will cut oil production to such an extent as gravely to imperil the economic growth of its customer nations.

6.36 The solution of all these problems is not possible without acceptance of a global energy policy. Such a policy must have, as its centre-piece, an accommodation between the oil-exporting and oil-importing countries. This accommodation would involve commitments by both sets of countries: by the major oil-exporting countries to agree not to reduce supplies arbitrarily unless circumstances are beyond their control; by the major oil-importing countries to hold oil-imports to ceilings below those agreed by IEA member countries, and to set and monitor strict conservation standards on the consumption of energy in its main end-uses (particularly that of petroleum products), with penalties to be applied where such standards are not reached; and by both oil-exporting and oil-importing countries to set real prices of crude petroleum and petroleum products in such a way as to avoid unpredictable and sudden, sharp increases, but at levels which give incentives for increased production as well as encouraging greater conservation. In addition, a global energy policy will have to incorporate a mechanism to effect greater investment in the exploration, production and transport of energy with present technologies – particularly in the production of petroleum and of nuclear energy within the present energy-deficient developing countries – as well as in R & D into new technologies for the production, conversion and utilisation of energy – especially that of renewable sources.

6.37 The opportunity presented by the UN Special Session on Development should be taken to instil into all parties the necessity of joining forces in

1. See BP Policy Review Unit Brief: *Oil Crisis . . . . . . Again?* (September 1979).

order to transform a potential energy crisis into a new opportunity for co-operation in the global interest. A concordat is needed between the industrialised countries (both market economy and centrally planned), OPEC and other developing countries in order to implement a global energy arrangement. But we wish to emphasise that such a concordat is possible only if it forms part of an agreement on the broad range of issues in the North-South dialogue.

# 7. Other Development Problems

7.1 In the foregoing chapters of this Report we have dealt with issues of special relevance to the current world economic situation – balance of payments deficits, protectionism, inflation and energy. Most other items on the North-South agenda have been so recently and fully treated in the Brandt Commission's report that we do not think it necessary to cover them again. But there are three on which we believe we have something useful to add. One is the problem of attaining a higher rate of official development assistance. The second is the problem of assuring adequate minimum food supplies for the world's poor. The third is the broad area of commodity problems. We have decided to confine this chapter to these three from among the whole range of other development issues. But we allow ourselves a final word each on manufacturing as a key element in the process of development and on the economic waste of the arms race.

### (a) Official Development Assistance

7.2 We begin with official development assistance. The record over the past decade is disappointing and the prospects for the future are not encouraging.

7.3 At the end of the 1970s official development aid from the industrialised countries was on a scale no greater than 0.35 per cent of GNP, exactly half of the target of 0.7 per cent agreed at the beginning of the decade and endorsed by the Brandt Commission for achievement by 1985.

7.4 There has been no sign that the industrialised countries will now seek to make a greater effort. Nearly all of them are struggling with high rates of inflation which dispose them to reduce rather than expand demand, especially demand abroad where this involves additional government spending. Most of them can also point to large external deficits as evidence that they can grant more aid to other countries only if they engage in additional borrowing abroad. Under these circumstances, they feel it necessary to limit additional aid to developing countries and to offer more only in exceptional cases.

7.5 So negative an approach to aid is not without its dangers to the industrialised countries themselves. The arguments for limiting aid on budgetary and balance of payments grounds are not compelling. Inflation does not prevent governments from continuing to spend on purposes they regard as important: the changes contemplated are on a limited scale in relation to the continuing level of government expenditure; indeed they are in a sense marginal. What governments decide to finance depends on the priority they attach to the benefits accruing: so that if they refuse to increase aid, that tells us more about the relative importance they attach to aid than about their fears of aggravating inflation. The case for more aid should rest on a view of the longer-term relationship between the developing and the developed countries rather than on the short-term conjuncture or the medium-term need to keep inflation under control.

7.6 The same is equally true of balance of payments fears. The industrialised countries may have special difficulties over the next year or two in avoiding external deficits and may reasonably hesitate to add to these difficulties. But again the fundamental question concerns the priority they attach to the various imports they continue to make in relation to the aid required by the developing countries.

7.7 To put the point in the most direct way, if aid were regarded as a form of defence expenditure that had to be financed on an increasing scale for the good of the country (or of the world economy), is it to be expected that governments would be deterred from supplying more aid by fears of inflation or concern for the balance of payments?

7.8 The answer would appear to be: to some extent, yes, but in the last resort, no. Economic difficulties do act as a constraint even on expenditure that would normally enjoy very high priority, and there are some kinds of expenditure that would be likely to intensify the difficulties. But if the OECD countries act together in granting additional aid it is doubtful whether their collective external deficit with the rest of the world would be much affected. Most of the extra aid supplied in the form of finance would flow back to the industrialised countries. Some of it might be used to service or repay existing debt. Most of it would be spent on goods supplied by the industrialised countries. If it took the form of tied loans, there would be no net change in the donor's balance of payments since both sides of the international accounts would expand equally. If the aid were not tied, there might be some shift in the balances of payments of the different OECD countries, depending on which contributed more in aid than they received again in orders; there might be among the less fortunate donors some that found special difficulty in handling external deficits or in making the adjustments necessary to keep them within manageable limits. So it is not possible completely to discount the balance of payments problem on the grounds that it would sort itself out. But if some means could be found of providing for special cases among the donors, the difficulties could be more easily surmounted.

7.9 The question whether current high rates of inflation constitute an obstacle to a larger aid effort or whether, on the contrary, the prospect of severe recession makes such an aid effort positively desirable as a stimulus to economic activity raises more complex analytical issues. Those who take the latter view and believe that many of the industrialised countries already suffer from excess capacity and deficiency of demand are likely to view the generation of additional demand from the developing countries as a welcome pump-priming mechanism. If the additional demand generated by extra aid took shape as a stream of orders from the developing countries for capital goods and other manufactures, it could be regarded as a form of international public-works, of which the benefits were shared between the recipients of the aid and the producers in the industrialised countries.

7.10 However, the view that what the industrialised countries are at present suffering from is a deficiency of aggregate effective demand in the Keynesian sense is strongly disputed by many knowledgeable observers. On their view, additional aid would certainly be inflationary unless it was financed by additional taxation. On either view, advocates of a greater aid effort would need to prove their point that more aid, whether financed from taxation or from expansion of money supply, is preferable to more domestic government expenditure. In other words, in the short-run the case for a larger aid effort must rest on public expenditure priorities; it derives little if any support from macro-economic demand management considerations except under conditions of deep depression. This conclusion is not inconsistent with the general proposition that, if there is agreement on other grounds that aid should be increased, countries have less reason to be deterred from giving effect to that agreement when they have resources to spare, particularly in those sectors of the economy towards which the demand of the recipient countries will tend to flow.

7.11 If the aid provided by the industrialised countries laid the basis for an expansion in the supply of primary produce, it might offer other advantages. As argued earlier, an important element in the inflationary process is the tendency for raw materials and agricultural produce to rise sharply in price when industrial recovery puts pressure on the supply. Action to make the supply more elastic could be an important contribution to reducing the danger of inflation and weakening the constraint it imposes on renewed growth, to the mutual benefit of developed and developing countries.

7.12 Finally, we must consider the medium- and long-term interest of the developed countries in the expansion of the economies of the South. Aid, or indeed any transfer of real resources, from the North to the South can and does increase the demand of the South for imports from the North and could also in many cases increase the South's exports to the North. The large-scale transfer of resources from the North to the South could therefore serve to expand international trade, which is more often than not an engine of growth for all participating countries.

7.13 While the least developed countries in particular and the low income countries in general (with their per capita incomes of less than $300) are the most deserving of concessionary flows of aid, there are also large areas of poverty in both the lower-middle and middle-income developing countries – both those qualifying for resources from the International Development Association, that is, with a per capita income (at present) of less than $581, and those not so qualifying.

7.14 High rates of economic growth over the past two or three decades in much of the Third World have failed to lift the standard of life of hundreds of millions who continue to live in extreme poverty in the poorest countries and even among the bottom 40 per cent in countries that have achieved substantial overall economic growth. The average performance of developing countries conceals wide disparities, ranging from a small group which, because they are major oil producers or because they have established their economies on a path of rapid self-sustaining growth, are approaching or even beginning to surpass some of those of the North, through a middle group of varying experience, to a large number of very poor small countries and a few low-income slowly-growing countries with very large populations. Even as these poorer countries are trying to accelerate their growth, their needs are also increasing apace, with continuing rapid population growth and a continuing revolution of rising expectations.

7.15 The core of the problem of poverty in the poorer countries of the Third World remains, despite vigorous strides in industrial development in many of them, the agricultural sector on which most of their populations continue to depend for their livelihood. The 'Green Revolution' has not so far fulfilled for rice, the high hopes which its earlier successes with maize and wheat had held out. New varieties evolved in international research centres have turned out to require much adaptive research in individual countries, and even regions within countries, and effective administration of extension to bring the new technology to the farmers before they can be relied on to sustain a steady rise in yields. The requisite research and administrative capacity in turn does not develop much ahead of the overall socio-economic development of each country.

7.16 It is also becoming clear, as we have explained, that food production alone is not the whole answer to the problem of hunger. Even rapid growth of food production will not eliminate malnutrition and periodic famine if the poor lack the money to buy the food. To raise nutritional standards, efforts to raise food production must be accompanied by adequate growth of entitlements, produced income and income supplements, of the undernourished poor. Both the improvement in farm productivity and the institutional changes in the rural social structure which are needed are primarily a matter for national policies and national effort in the developing countries themselves. But there is scope for international collective action to help these countries in their onslaught on the problem of poverty.

7.17 In the long-run, development is a necessary if not a sufficient condition for the elimination of poverty. In so far as official development aid has aimed at providing technical assistance and training as well as economic infrastructure, such as roads, irrigation, power and other such projects, it has undoubtedly contributed and will need to continue to contribute to the alleviation of poverty in the long-run. But the case for more aid for these broad purposes has lost some of its power of appeal, and a major reason is almost certainly widespread doubt among public opinion in the North, whether such aid is always, or indeed ever, effectively used to help the poor now. Such views may have little basis in fact, and a better understanding of the role that aid plays may help to dispel misconceptions. Meanwhile, however, they act as a political barrier to a more substantial aid effort by the developed countries.

7.18 It is our belief that ODA clearly directed at the alleviation of poverty, within the framework of a comprehensive development strategy, offers the best chance of enlisting public support in the North, and thus of raising the total development assistance effort above the current average of 0.35 per cent of GNP somewhat closer to the 0.7 per cent target. We would argue that, in this sense, additional ODA consisting of specific poverty programmes would be in the mutual interest of governments in the North and South.

7.19 In deciding on the detailed content of such a programme, the North must closely cooperate with, and indeed be largely guided by, the South. It is for the governments of the Third World to suggest what criteria of allocation of ODA among countries and what projects, policy measures and safeguards are most likely to promote the objective of alleviation of poverty. The following criteria may commend themselves:

(i) Priority for countries with a per capita income below the IDA level, at present $ 581, and particularly for the least developed and poorer countries with a per capita income below $300, since any effective use of ODA in countries so poor has a high degree of probability of benefiting poor people.

(ii) ODA for other countries should focus on specific poverty programmes, for example for the further reduction of infant mortality, for the elimination of debilitating tropical diseases, for the improvement of nutrition, housing and water-supply in rural and urban poverty areas, for comprehensive primary education opportunities, for employment-creating public-works programmes, selected in such a way as to combine as far as possible the immediate alleviation of distress with longer-term improvement of income-earning capacity of the beneficiary groups. In many cases it would be essential to include the provision of economic infrastructure. Thus such projects could be both short- and long-term in their purpose and contribute both directly and indirectly to poverty redressal.

Experience has shown that even schemes with clearly poverty-oriented objectives may fail if too large a proportion of the funds made available is absorbed by donor and recipient bureaucracies. To find practicable means of limiting this drain is an important part of the task.

7.20 Over the next two decades these areas of poverty need a high rate of investment in large-scale physical assets, in both the directly productive areas such as agriculture and industry and in economic and social infrastructure, to bring about high rates of economic growth; this is essential if the provision of the basic needs of the masses of the people are to be met on a sustainable basis over a long period of time. In other words, the meeting of basic needs represents both consumption and investment, but it is not the only form of investment required if the economy is to grow rapidly and so achieve a self-sustaining economic development and structural transformation.

7.21 The element of time, however, is crucial in the whole issue of meeting basic needs, as it is in many areas of economics. It makes a considerable difference whether the government of a country or an aid donor to that country is aiming to meet the basic needs of the poor in five years' time or in twenty years' time. In many of the poorest countries there may be so few available resources that it may not be possible to meet the bare physiological needs of the poor in five years; but if a steady expansion of resources becomes available through the pursuit of complementary policies of economic growth and structural transformation, this goal might be attainable in, say, twenty years' time. This point has been put very well in the Address of the President of the World Bank to the 1979 Meeting of the Board of Governors of that institution:

> "As I have argued before, this requires that the traditional growth approach be supplemented by a direct concern with the basic needs of the poor. This is not a prescription for global philanthropy. Nor should it confuse means and ends, and rule out means that may be necessary to achieve the objective – industrialisation, for example, or investment for economic infrastructure. Nor should it merely treat the symptom rather than the causes of poverty. Such gross over-simplifications can bring the very concept of an attack on poverty into disrepute. And they often have".

### (b) Food

7.22 In spite of improvements in the overall world food situation since the 1973-74 food crisis, the world food security situation remains precarious. Very little progress has been made in establishing a dependable system of world food security – one that would ensure that small changes in availability at the world, regional or national level, or in the command over food supplies at national or local level, do not worsen the already extensive incidence of hunger and malnutrition.

7.23 During the 1970s, food production in developing countries rose on average by 3 per cent annually. But in many developing countries, production increases failed to match population growth. Production was particularly disappointing in countries with the most serious food problems – the 46 Most Seriously Affected (MSA) countries – a category which, significantly, was designated as such after the first round of steep fuel price increases in 1973-74 and which the FAO and the World Food Council still find useful for assessing the world food security situation. High fuel prices have aggravated the food problem. They have impaired the capacity of these countries to purchase food even in cases where the relative dependence on imported food has not increased. Fertiliser prices have also been moving up with fuel prices.

7.24 In volume terms, food imports into developing countries increased by 7 per cent annually during the 1970s. Cereal imports, which comprised about one-half of the food imports, increased from 52 million tons a year in 1971-1973 to 85 million tons in 1979-80. The problem of increasing food imports and declining self-sufficiency highlights the more fundamental issue that food production is not making an adequate contribution to economic development.

7.25 In recent years, high priority has been given to food production in external assistance. While higher proportions of resources have flowed to agriculture, total resource flows have been increasing too sluggishly to make the required impact. Since the food problem is concentrated in low-income countries, and food production tends to attract little private foreign investment, concessional capital flows are of critical importance.

7.26 One favourable development in recent years has been significant increases in fertiliser consumption in developing countries. It is extremely important that this trend does not falter because of balance of payment problems and higher fertiliser prices. Assistance must be made available to the poorest countries in order to ensure that fertiliser consumption is maintained in periods of high prices or other adverse circumstances. In this connection we note the valuable contribution being made through the FAO in providing fertiliser on a concessionary basis to these countries and recognise the continuing need for such an arrangement.

7.27 The international community is planning special programmes and accelerated action to assist the 30 countries designated as least developed. Since most of these countries are also food priority countries, we urge particular attention be given to their food problems. A recent estimate shows that although the least developed countries have 18 per cent of the arable land in developing countries, they were responsible for only 3.3 per cent of the fertiliser used. Fertiliser use becomes especially important to intensify production in the many countries which are short of land. Some countries have unutilised land which, if there were roads, could be brought into use. Many of these least developed countries depend on rain-fed agriculture and the installation of irrigation facilities is also an urgent need.

7.28 Production increases alone will not solve the problems of hunger and malnutrition. As we have pointed out in Chapter 2, distribution considerations are very important. Famines can ensue where availability has not declined, because of changes in the ability of different sections of the population to command food. Food being a basic necessity, policies are required not only to prevent significant changes in the ability of vulnerable sections to command it, but also to increase such ability on the part of people suffering from malnutrition. In other words, effort has to be concentrated not just on increasing supply, but also on the pattern of demand. This is important not just for humanitarian reasons, but in order to raise the productive capacity and energies of underfed people. What is often required is a redistribution both of income and of productive assets. Land reform to provide the basic means for larger sections to participate in food production could improve food distribution, apart from any effect it may have in increasing production through more intensive land use. Distribution could also be improved directly by increasing entitlement through the issue of food coupons, and through subsidised prices. Some countries are already taking action to improve food distribution by these means. We urge greater attention be paid in international and domestic policies to food distribution in order to ensure that economic changes do not adversely affect the entitlement of vulnerable populations.

7.29 In view of the wide extent of hunger and malnutrition we recognise the important role of food aid and the need for an expanded programme which would incorporate greater predictability through forward commitments. In its administration, however, particularly at the local level, such a programme must endeavour to minimise or eliminate disincentive effects on food production. Besides food aid, the other components of a dependable system of international food security must include reasonably stable grain prices, expanded storage capacity in developing countries, and international arrangements to ensure that food supplies are maintained to the poorest countries in periods of international shortage and local harvest failure.

### (c) Commodities

7.30 Commodity trade is of particular importance to the less industrialised developing countries. A large number of these still depend on one or two commodities for more than half of their export earnings. Slow progress in implementation of the Integrated Programme for Commodities (IPC) has been one of the major failures of international economic policy in the 1970s. Considering the importance of commodity exports for some of the poorest countries in the world, a world-wide programme to stabilise commodity markets remains a test of the collective will of the international community to create an effective framework for self-sustained economic development in the developing countries.

7.31 For developing countries, the turbulent economic conditions of recent years have helped highlight the adverse effects of violent fluctuations in commodity prices. Boom prices have added to inflationary pressures, while low prices have depressed producer incomes and aggravated balance of payments problems. Similarly, in analysis of inflationary trends in industrialised countries, movements in commodity prices are recognised as having played a significant part.

7.32 In view of the extensive treatment given to commodity problems in international fora in recent years, we confine ourselves to particular aspects which we feel deserve special attention in the light of recent developments. Following some comments on developments in price stabilisation arrangements, we focus on the areas covered by the Second Window of the Common Fund and on export earnings stabilisation. A few words only are needed to supplement what was said in earlier chapters about local processing and about oil and mineral exploration.

7.33 Very little progress has been made in setting up new International Commodity Agreements (ICAs) in the negotiations being undertaken under the IPC. So far, agreement has been reached to set up only one new ICA, that on natural rubber. In the meantime, negotiation to secure the continuation of one existing ICA – the International Cocoa Agreement – beyond its termination date of March 1980, has failed. The Common Fund will not become significant unless new ICAs are established.

7.34 The record of ICAs and of the negotiations to set them up has, on the whole, been disappointing. While these efforts must continue on the basis of the preparatory work and discussions now taking place, the time has come for some basic rethinking on appropriate stabilisation measures. Greater attention should be given to measures which are less complex and easier to administer. For instance, more use could be made of variable export taxes, adopted on a coordinated basis. Such taxes, levied at appropriate levels for raw materials and processed products, could also help to counteract the adverse effects of tariff escalation on domestic processing. There should be energetic efforts to establish the 10 core ICAs by 1985, the midpoint of the Third Development Decade.

7.35 Considerable dissatisfaction has been expressed at the amount of resources provided for the Common Fund. Part of the problem has been the unwillingness of governments to provide higher levels of capital subscriptions. If adequate finance is assured, the Fund could assist in the establishment of buffer-stock ICAs and in making their operation feasible. The Common Fund, as a new venture in commodity stabilisation, should be given full support by governments. It should be provided with the means to carry out effectively the agreed price stabilisation objectives.

*The Second Window*

7.36 The main functions envisaged for the Second Window of the Common Fund are R & D, productivity improvement, marketing, and vertical diversification. In the financing arrangements for the Window, it has been agreed that not less than $70 million will be provided from capital subscriptions and a target of $280 million has been set for voluntary contributions. Thus it is envisaged that the Window will have about $350 million.

7.37 We believe that the Second Window can, in important ways, supplement present commodity financing. Many activities are not funded adequately at present because they require action on a commodity-wide basis. Examples are generic market promotion, and R & D on new end-uses and basic production techniques. Some of the activities are suitable for action on a regional basis, where the costs can be shared. Improvements in simple processing technology, for example, could benefit many producing countries. The benefits of some R & D work flow to all producing countries and unless arrangements exist for the sharing of costs, they tend to be deterred. Market promotion and R & D have also suffered from the reluctance of international financial agencies to support them.

7.38 In the case of market promotion, information available shows that it is not as such financed by the World Bank or IDA. In the case of R & D, external financing has been concentrated on food products. No R & D has been financed for products facing competition from synthetics. Some financing has been undertaken on horizontal diversification, but the evidence available shows that appraisal of these projects has been too country-oriented and has not taken adequately into account wider international considerations. Thus, while in South Asia diversification from tea has been financed, in East Africa tea production has been encouraged in order to reduce dependence on coffee. While these seemingly contradictory projects may not be economically irrational if seen from a local vantage point, it is likely that if such projects had been initiated under the auspices of ICAs greater account would have been taken of the wider issues.

7.39 In the light of these considerations, we attach great importance to Second Window activities and do not regard them as mere appendages to the buffer-stock operations of the Common Fund. We see important roles for the Window in supporting projects which need the global commodity approach and also in encouraging other financial institutions to become interested in them.

7.40 Special efforts should be made to enable the Second Window to reach an effective level of operation. Its purpose could not be met only by voluntary contributions. It is going to need a higher level of obligatory financing. Meanwhile, however, the industrialised countries should ensure that the target of $280 million of voluntary contributions is reached.

*Export Earnings Stabilisation*

7.41 Commodity export earnings stabilisation schemes must play a stronger complementary role to price stabilisation ICAs. The IPC envisaged a larger role for export earnings stabilisation than now exists. However, the negotiations on the Common Fund have hitherto been given priority.

7.42 In recent years, significant improvements have been made in the two schemes in existence – the IMF Compensatory Financing Facility (CFF) and the more modest export earnings stabilisation scheme (Stabex) which forms part of the ACP/EEC Lome Convention. But there is widespread dissatisfaction with these limited efforts. Proposals have been put forward by West Germany and Sweden for global schemes that could complement the CFF but that would be commodity-related like Stabex. At UNCTAD V a resolution was adopted requesting the UNCTAD Secretariat to undertake a study on a proposal for a complementary facility, in consultation with the IMF.

7.43 The McIntyre Group's report[1] gave considerable attention to the question of improvement in the provision of compensatory financing. We are pleased to note that changes have been made in the CFF along the lines of the Group's recommendations in two respects – extension of the scheme to encompass invisible earnings and the greater accommodation of shortfalls by increasing the ceilings. We believe, however, that the CFF, because of the basic balance of payments orientation of IMF objectives, falls short of a required global commodities export earnings scheme in three respects:

(i) it is still limited to quotas and, therefore, often cannot provide compensation to the full extent of export shortfalls;

(ii) it is related to total export earnings and not specifically to commodity earnings and, therefore, does not respond to the particular needs of the commodities sector; and

(iii) it does not take into account balance of payments problems arising from sudden, sharp changes in the price of imports, for example some commodity imports such as food and fuel.

7.44 These are serious gaps in export earnings stabilisation. They require urgent attention. In case these changes cannot be incorporated in the CFF within the framework of IMF policies, earnest consideration should be given to establishing a separate but complementary facility.

7.45 We pointed in Chapter 4 to the scope for increased export earnings from commodities by enlarging domestic processing. There are some economic and policy changes, such as higher pollution standards in industrialised countries and the high cost of fuel, which are increasing the comparative

1. A final report by a Commonwealth Experts' Group, op. cit.

advantage of developing countries. We noted that escalating tariffs remain a serious barrier to relocating processing facilities. The problem is made worse by practices concerning freight rate charges. These result in higher transport costs for processed products.

7.46 But there are other constraints besides these artificial ones. Capital requirements are increasing. Moreover, the required capital and technology are often in the possession of transnational enterprises. Their location policy does not always conform closely to wider rational economic considerations nor to the urgent development needs of developing countries. A larger role in providing financing is therefore required of the international financial agencies. Other aspects demanding international attention are the development of technology appropriate to the circumstances of developing countries and marketing.

*Mineral Exploration*

7.47 According to World Bank estimates, about 80 per cent of total expenditure on exploration by market economy countries is concentrated in four developed countries, and this in spite of the higher probability of finding minerals in the largely unmapped undeveloped regions of the world. The tendency to exploit more costly resources affects the welfare of the whole world community, and has serious implications for assuring long-term supplies.

7.48 The problem is seen as 'political' risk, arising from nationalisation, the unilateral renouncement of contracts and demands for renegotiation of what in the eyes of the host country have come to be seen as inequitable terms. The issues here are substantially the same as in relation to oil exploration which we discussed in Chapter 6 (paragraphs 6.5-6.7). The suggestions we made there to bring about an improvement in the design of contracts for energy exploration could usefully be extended to other minerals.

### (d) Manufacturing

7.49 The relative roles of agriculture and industry in promoting development depend on such factors as the stage of development and resource endowment. It is important to recognise, however, the increasingly important role that must be played by manufacturing in the course of development and of the fast rate of expansion required if the usually small manufacturing sector is to make a significant impact on unemployment and underemployment. The small size of local markets gives freer access for the manufactured products of developing countries a crucial role in encouraging industrialisation.

7.50 Developing countries are responsible now for only about 8 per cent of world production of manufactured goods. While commentators have stressed the difficulties involved in achieving the UNIDO Lima target of a 25 per cent share for developing countries in world production of manufactured goods by the year 2000, and have queried the usefulness of such a target, we believe that it has the merit of highlighting the challenges involved and the great efforts required if developing countries are to achieve satisfactory growth rates. The implication of overall growth targets for the expansion of the industrial sector indicates the sustained effort required: to secure increased investment, including foreign investment in industrial infrastructure and plants; to promote the transfer and indigenous development of appropriate technology; to eliminate restrictive practices on technology transfer arrangements and in trading policies of transnational corporations; to improve trade and adjustment policies in industrialised countries in order to facilitate smooth industrial restructuring in these countries and the rapid expansion of manufacturing and processing industries in developing countries; and to adopt efficient and sufficiently outward-looking domestic industrial policies in the developing countries.

7.51 The industrialised countries could also identify specific labour-intensive areas of production, which do not enjoy a comparative advantage vis-a-vis developing countries, with a view to encouraging the movement of resources out of these industries within a definite time-schedule. Industrialised Commonwealth countries in particular should make firm commitments to phase-out protection of manufactures which can be more competitively produced by developing Commonwealth countries within an appropriate time-frame in graduated stages, over the medium- and longer-term.

**(e) Disarmament and Development**

7.52 Aid from governments of the richer industrialised countries of the world to their less developed neighbours is in competition with all other objects of government expenditure in the donor countries. But there are good grounds for singling out defence as being in a special sense competitive. Any country's security depends not only on its expenditure on armaments but on the circumstances in other countries that dispose them to take up aggressive attitudes, and on the success with which these countries can be brought to collaborate in mutually advantageous pursuits. It may be more important to have thriving neighbours, to enjoy satisfactory trading relationships with them and to promote their development by adding to the resources at their disposal, than to spend to the uttermost on defence. Yet as matters now stand, of all forms of government expenditure in the advanced countries, both those with market and with centrally planned economies, defence makes the largest, or nearly the largest call on resources while overseas aid makes one of the smallest. On the average, twenty times as much goes on military expenditure as on aid for development in the market economies (and the ratio is much larger still in the centrally planned economies). Thus there is a choice between, say, an extra 5 per cent on defence and doubling the provision for aid; and it is not unreasonable to ask which would be likely to make the greater contribution to security.

7.53 The question gains added point when looked at in global terms. Military spending by the world as a whole now amounts to $450 billion a year, or more than a quarter of the entire income of the developing countries. However much each country may seek to justify this expenditure, the world economy is the loser, not the gainer from the heavy burden it involves. It absorbs resources on a vast scale that could be used, in a world where peace was assured, to accelerate the slow improvement in living standards. Indeed the resources so absorbed, since they include a large proportion of the world's scientists and technologists, and much of the most up-to-date and novel equipment, could play a particularly useful role at the frontiers of economic development either in the advanced or in the less developed countries. If this is so, it must be true also that the diversion of these resources to military purposes is a serious constraint on current rates of growth. It may well be no accident that countries like Germany and Japan, which have not been free to expand their defence budgets, have enjoyed remarkably rapid rates of economic growth.

7.54 But of course it is not only in the advanced countries that defence expenditure represents a heavy call on resources that might go to benefit development. The developing countries (including the poorest among them) also spend billions of dollars on armaments, nearly all imported from abroad. They too might do well to consider whether such expenditure is the best guarantee of their security and whether a more whole-hearted concentration on economic development, supported by funds diverted from military expenditure, might not in the end be more effective.

7.55 We are well aware that a general reduction in arms spending in the world will be difficult to achieve without new measures for collective international security. Whatever the difficulties of attaining that goal, and we do not intend to minimise them, there is little doubt that a purposeful pursuit of conditions for political and economic justice everywhere in the world could in itself create a more secure international atmosphere, and help to divert scarce and valuable world resources from destructive uses to the satisfaction of urgent human needs.

# 8. Summary and Conclusions

### Development and Crisis

8.1 This Report has been written at a time when adverse trends in the world economy combine to constitute a veritable world economic crisis: co-existence of two-digit inflation and high unemployment in the developed market economies, slowdown of economic growth in all parts of the world, and disequilibria in balances of payments of a magnitude scarcely conceivable a decade ago. There is anxious questioning whether we are on the brink of an economic disaster comparable to the Great Depression of the 1930s.

8.2 Our concern has been chiefly with the implications of the world economic crisis for the developing countries of the Third World. The burden of our argument has been that it is always the poor who are most vulnerable. The consequences of inflation and recession, of high oil prices and balance of payments deficits are grave enough for the high-income industrialised countries. They are liable to be catastrophic for the developing countries, and most of all for the poorest and least developed among them.

8.3 At the outset we have thought it necessary to warn that further compression of incomes in developing countries would in many cases mean reduced ability to buy even the minimum necessities of life, especially food, and would therefore accentuate poverty and starvation. The lesson of history is that starvation can be caused not only by a fall in food supply but also by such economic disturbances as balance of payments deficits, unemployment and inflation. The asymmetry between the effects of these problems on the populations of the developed countries and on wide sections of the developing countries adds to the current crisis a perspective that can be ignored only at the cost of a sharp accentuation of poverty and starvation. The urgency of preventing sudden contractions in economic activity within the developing countries must therefore be viewed in more ways than merely in terms of sluggish economic performance.

8.4 Many of the problems in the international economy cannot be solved by nations acting on their own or in small groups. Attempts by individual countries to maximise their gains or minimise their losses in isolation may reduce the welfare of all. Unfortunately, that is the direction in which things are moving. There is now a dangerous tendency among the world's leading nations to seek their own solutions. More urgent even than agreement on particular problems is progress towards re-establishing rules for collective decision-making. In making in this Report a plea for collective action by North and South to cushion the impact of adversity and making a number of specific recommendations, which are summarised in the following paragraphs, we have deliberately avoided setting our sights too high, in the hope that the measures we have proposed will be recognised on all sides as being clearly in the enlightened long-run self-interest of North and South alike.

**The Balance of Payments Problem**

8.5 The financing of balance of payments deficits of oil-importing developing countries will remain one of the most critical issues, particularly over the next two or three years. There are doubts about the capacity and willingness of official and private sources of external finance to provide these countries with funds on the required scale. It is impossible to be precise about the level of financing needed, but it appears that the net oil-importing developing countries, particularly the low-income countries and those of the middle-income countries which are not in a position to expand their exports of manufactures, will together require amounts in the range of $5-$10 billion, beyond those ordinarily likely to be forthcoming from external sources, in 1980 and 1981.

8.6 If these deficits are not financed, there will be a serious compression of real imports and a substantial cutback in the already low growth rates of net oil-importing developing countries. This would have adverse effects not only for developing countries but for the developed countries as well. If global economic activity is to be sustained, there is urgent need to provide additional financing mechanisms to limit exchange rate instability, to facilitate larger flows of commercial funds to non-oil countries, and to increase official sources of financing for those not in a position to borrow from the commercial banks. In particular, to meet immediate needs it should be possible for the World Bank to make fuller use of programme lending and for the IMF to establish a new facility which would lend to the poorer developing countries on first credit tranche conditions.

8.7 The least developed countries and some of the low-income countries facing a serious debt situation would not be able to afford finance even on Third Window terms. For these we recommend that a special programme be established just as soon as possible to provide increased official assistance from bilateral and multilateral sources to meet balance of payments deficits. We also suggest that OPEC consider giving these countries a rebate on oil prices for a limited period, say five years.

8.8 The immediate need for balance of payments support shades into the need to bring about structural adjustments in these economies. Longer-term programme lending will be required in larger amounts for this purpose.

8.9 We strongly recommend that negotiations between interested parties should commence without delay to take the following steps : first, the provision of facilities for reserve diversification by the oil-exporting countries, whether through off-market transactions which would, in effect, create a tier of secondary reserve assets for the participating central banks or through the proposed IMF Substitution Account; second, the on-lending of such funds via the IMF to developing countries on suitable terms for financing their deficits; and third, consideration of possible ways of making this on-lending process the starting point for long-term programme financing. A feasible mechanism might be the negotiation between governments of appropriate guarantee arrangements. This could later be given permanent form by converting the guarantees into the callable capital (in the sense of a system of limited 'joint and several guarantees') of a lending institution.

8.10 It would be possible to give effect to the financing arrangements we have in mind through existing institutions: the World Bank Group on the one hand and an enlarged OPEC Special Fund on the other. This would require a relaxation of the rules under which the World Bank engages in programme lending and would also require a substantial addition to the resources made available to IDA. Alternatively, the financing arrangements might provide the starting point for a new institution such as the World Development Fund proposed by the Brandt Commission.

8.11 The amount which could be eventually raised in the manner suggested above would be very large – figures of up to $20 billion have been proposed for the OPEC Development Agency alone – and it would be reasonable to expect that a fund or funds of this magnitude, involving developed countries as well, would be in a position to widen its range of activities as compared, for example, with a transformed OPEC Special Fund. It would be for consideration whether these activities should be administered by a common agency, the sums raised under guarantees provided by OPEC and the developed countries being pooled, or whether it would be preferable to retain separate agencies working in close collaboration. Whatever is done by OPEC there is an opportunity and a very real need for an initiative by the developed countries in the mutual interest of both developed and developing countries.

**Protectionism and Structural Adjustment**

8.12 The present trend to increasing protectionism in developed countries constitutes one of the most serious threats to the structural changes in world production and trade that are necessary for continuing growth and development. The new protectionism, which takes the form usually of 'orderly marketing arrangements' and 'voluntary export restraints', is directed largely against labour-intensive products, some of which make up a substantial proportion of exports of developing countries. By slowing down growth of income and structural change in the newly industrialising countries, it adversely affects market prospects and development throughout the Third World. The whole process of economic development is being severely affected by restricted access for many first-stage manufacturing products. In view of the small domestic markets in many developing countries, expanding foreign markets for their products are important to these countries.

8.13 Protectionism adversely affects the economic health of the North as much as the South. Protectionism has been rationalised by the belief that unemployment rates in developed countries are highly sensitive to competition from developing countries, but the evidence does not support this. On the contrary, such trade has tended to have a positive effect on employment in industrialised countries. Any labour displacement is insignificant compared to the effects of technical change or of competition from other industrialised countries. The extra cost of protectionist measures to consumers in industrialised countries has been considerable.

8.14 We support the OECD's emphasis on "the centrality of trade in a mutual interest agenda". Primary responsibility here lies with the North and the most general recipe is the adoption of positive adjustment policies.

8.15 The developing countries should maintain political pressure on the industrialised countries for freer access to their markets. Beyond this, the developing countries should take the maximum advantage of openings for liberalisation presented by the Tokyo Round. They should participate actively in the future management of the new codes and in the material benefits which can be achieved under the improved rules of the codes.

8.16 One of the most serious obstacles to the liberalisation of trade is abuse by the industrialised countries of 'safeguard measures'. Safeguard actions should be permitted only under limited and clearly defined conditions. Such measures should be subject to automatic reductions over time and to multilateral control and surveillance, and be linked with the adoption of positive policies of industrial adjustment.

8.17 Of immediate concern to most developing countries is the incidence of tariff escalation, which deters the location and relocation of feasible processing in raw material exporting developing countries. The reduction of tariff escalation remains of great importance to these countries.

8.18 Another area of concern is protectionism in agricultural products, which remains pervasive and deep-rooted. Little progress on these products was made in the Tokyo Round of multilateral trade negotiations and a more determined effort at liberalisation is needed. Developing countries should join forces with like-minded developed countries in demanding freer agricultural trade. A commitment should be sought for the complete removal by the end of 1981 of all barriers to imports into industrialised countries from developing countries of non-competing agricultural products. For other farm products special arrangements are required to facilitate access of exports from developing countries while longer-term efforts are made to liberalise and restructure agricultural trade.

8.19 The centrally planned economies constitute a large potential market for the exports of developing countries. Centralised decision-making in these countries provides the opportunity for policy decisions which could quickly expand purchases of the exports of developing countries.

8.20 The expected lower growth rates of the industrialised countries in the foreseeable future, as well as the rise of protectionism, make it necessary for developing countries to pay special attention to opportunities for expanding trade among themselves. To realise this potential, provision of the related infrastructural arrangements must be given priority attention and trade policy should be reoriented accordingly. Global and binding trade preference arrangements among developing countries – now possible under GATT – deserve the support of the international community.

8.21 The time is ripe for a comprehensive examination of the whole problem and negotiation of improved access for the products of the developing countries in the markets of the developed countries. The global round of North-South negotiations which is to take place in 1981 provides an opportunity. The framework for such negotiations should be a priority subject at the UN Special Session on Development.

**The Inflation Problem**

8.22 During the 1970s inflation came increasingly to dominate the international scene, and its acceleration had serious harmful effects on growth. Whatever the causes of this acceleration, its harmful effects have been aggravated by changes in the attitudes of governments, which have become increasingly willing to acquiesce in a slowing down of growth as a means of keeping inflation under control.

8.23 There are no universal or agreed solutions to inflation and the correct mix of policies, monetary and non-monetary, can only be decided by governments on the basis of their local circumstances. But we do wish to emphasise that whatever may be the appropriate mix of policies from a national point of view, due account must be taken of the effects of these policies on other countries. It is important that, in their efforts to counter inflation, governments do not lose sight of their other obligations to one another.

**The Energy Issue**

8.24 Energy emerged during the 1970s as one of the dominant issues for the remainder of this century. World attention focused primarily on the sharp increases in oil prices in 1973-74 and 1979-80, and on the critical limits to petroleum as a major future source of energy. To the extent that the exploration and development of alternative sources of energy are accelerated as a consequence of this, the global economy will benefit over the long-term.

8.25 There are immense reserves of fossil and nuclear fuels remaining to be proved but in most developing countries their exploration has been held back by lack of adequate investment. In order to promote a fair sharing of the gains between external investors and host countries, we recommend the wider adoption in concession agreements of a 'resource rent tax' principle and other similar arrangements. Among these might be provision of official funds on concessional terms to assist developing countries to survey and assess their countries' energy resource potential before entering into contracts with external investors. A further expansion of the World Bank's current energy programme would be desirable. In the case of energy development we believe the most effective role for official multilateral facilities is to act as a catalyst and in other ways to reassure external investors.

8.26 As regards the development of energy potential, one important aspect is to raise the energy recovery factor through greater employment of advanced technologies (for example secondary and tertiary recovery of oil). No less important in the long-term is the fostering of R & D into new sources of energy, although most of these are unlikely to make a significant contribution to world energy supplies for several decades. Meanwhile, developing countries need greater technical assistance to help them establish or strengthen their present capacity to adapt and use conventional energy technologies, especially to minimise environmental hazards in the use of the only two alternatives to oil and natural gas which are economic on a large-scale, namely coal and nuclear energy.

8.27 Apart from increasing energy supplies, it is necessary to take measures to enhance energy conservation. To influence consumers' energy-using practices an appropriate pricing policy for the consumption of energy, especially of petroleum products, is indispensable and urgent, above all in the major oil-consuming countries. Mandatory fuel standards may be a useful supplement to such a pricing policy.

8.28 There is considerable potential for conserving energy consumption by applying improved technologies for energy conversion, distribution and utilisation, as around two-thirds of the caloric content is lost in these processes. Increasing public awareness of the progress of energy technologies, and of the ability to acquire, absorb and supply them, is crucial to energy conservation. It demands not only greater efforts by national governments but also increased international cooperation to establish or strengthen energy training facilities and R & D institutions in developing countries.

8.29 There is need for a global energy policy. Its centre-piece must be an accommodation between the oil exporting and importing countries, involving commitments by both. The major oil-exporting countries should not reduce supplies arbitrarily and should set real prices of crude petroleum in such a way as to avoid unpredictable and sudden, sharp increases. The major oil-importing countries should hold oil-imports to ceilings below those recently agreed by IEA member countries, set and monitor strict conservation standards on the consumption of energy in its main end-uses, with penalties where standards are not reached, and set energy prices to final consumers at levels which give incentives for increased energy production as well as encourage greater economy in its use. But we wish to emphasise that such a global energy policy can only be part of an agreement on a broad range of issues in the North-South dialogue.

**Other Development Problems**

8.30 From the large North-South agenda, we have selected five other topics for special and immediate attention.

*(a) Official Development Assistance*

8.31 The urgency of increasing levels of Official Development Assistance (ODA) has never been greater than now. The balance of payments problems of many developing countries are more acute, prospects for growth of their exports are threatened by rising protectionism, and their capacity to finance even minimum requirements of essential imports has deteriorated sharply. At the beginning of the decade of the 1970s, the developed countries committed themselves to an ODA target of 0.7 per cent of their GNP; at the end of the decade actual transfers stood at one-half of this figure – about 0.35 per cent of GNP. A greater effort must be made in the 1980s to reach the target to which developed countries are already committed.

8.32 We do not believe that the present concern about inflation is in itself a plausible justification for delaying action on stepping-up flows of ODA. While we appreciate the importance that many governments attach to the reduction of government expenditures, governments do continue to spend increasing amounts on purposes that they regard as important and to which they attach priority. A deepening of recession would strengthen the case for larger unilateral transfers to the developing countries.

8.33 The basic causes of poverty cannot be removed without structural transformation and sustained economic growth, requiring high rates of investment not only in small-scale projects in agricultural and rural sectors, but also in large-scale economic and social infrastructure and industrial projects. Aid must continue to facilitate the adoption and financing of such multi-faceted programmes for the removal of the basic causes of poverty. But a programme which specifically focuses on the poorest countries and on poverty groups and regions in other developing countries within the framework of a comprehensive development strategy would, in our view, offer the best prospect of evoking a positive response in developed countries for an immediate substantial increase in ODA.

### *(b) Food*

8.34 In spite of improvements in the overall world food situation since the 1973-74 food crisis, the world food security situation remains precarious. Very little progress has been made in establishing a dependable system of world food security. It is important to maintain the momentum of efforts to increase food production. Since the food problem is centred in the poorer developing countries, external capital flows and particularly concessional capital flows are of importance. As regards food distribution, effort has to be concentrated not only on increasing supplies but also on ensuring for all sufficient command over food supplies. This can be facilitated through a redistribution of income and of productive assets (for example land) and by policies which assure vulnerable sections of adequate entitlements.

8.35 Besides measures to increase food production, through improvement in agricultural technology, water control and management, and supplies of fertiliser and other inputs, a dependable system of international food security must include reasonably stable grain prices, expanded storage capacity in developing countries, food aid, and international arrangements to ensure that supplies are maintained to the poorest countries in periods of international shortage and local harvest failure.

### *(c) The Commodity Problem*

8.36 Considering the importance of commodity exports for some of the poorest countries, a world-wide programme to stabilise commodity markets remains a test of the will of the international community to create an effective framework for self-sustained economic development in the developing countries.

8.37 The Common Fund should be given full support by governments. It should be provided with the means to carry out effectively the agreed price stabilisation objectives. In the establishment of International Commodity Agreements (ICAs), attention should be given to simplicity and ease of administration. For instance, more use could be made of variable export taxes, adopted on a coordinated basis. There should be energetic efforts to establish the 10 core ICAs by 1985, the mid-point of the Third Development Decade. Steps should be taken to ensure that the Second Window reaches an effective level of operation. Its purpose could not be met only by voluntary contributions. But the industrialised countries should ensure at least that the target of $280 million of voluntary contributions is reached.

8.38 There are significant gaps in export earnings stabilisation. If measures to fill these gaps cannot be incorporated in the Compensatory Financing Facility of the IMF, serious consideration should be given to establishing a separate but complementary facility.

8.39 There should be a greater involvement of developing countries in the processing and distribution of their commodities. This requires the international agencies to play a larger role in the provision of finance, and greater attention to be paid to the removal of illiberal trade policies and of restrictive business practices.

### *(d) Manufacturing*

8.40 Manufacturing has a crucial role to play in the economic development of most developing countries. Freer access to the markets of the developed countries is therefore vital. The Lima target of a 25 per cent share for developing countries in world production of manufactured goods by the year 2000 presents a challenge and calls for a sustained effort to secure increased investment flows and technological transfers to these countries, the elimination of restrictive trading practices of transnational corporations and the improvement of trade and adjustment policies in industrialised countries. To this end, industrialised countries could identify and encourage the movement of resources out of the particular industries in which developing countries have greater comparative advantage. The Commonwealth developed countries could take a lead by setting a definite time-frame for such a programme within the Commonwealth on a bilateral or multilateral basis.

### *(e) Disarmament and Development*

8.41 The diversion of enormous resources to military purposes throughout the world is a serious constraint on rates of economic growth. A purposeful pursuit of conditions for political and economic justice everywhere in the world could create a more secure international atmosphere, and help to divert scarce and valuable world resources from destructive uses to the satisfaction of urgent human needs.

## In Conclusion

8.42 We are convinced that many of the problems of the international economy cannot be solved by nations acting on their own or in small groups. The present tendency of the world's leading nations to seek solutions individually, with too little reference to the global dimension, is a cause of serious concern. The interdependence of the world economy is now so strong that there would be a good case for collective action even in times of prosperity and growth; in the crisis situation now prevailing the case for joint action is compelling.

8.43 Change is inevitable. The issue, as we see it, is whether the structural changes and adjustments necessary to solve the current economic crisis and the problems of development will be accompanied by economic confusion and chaos, with each nation struggling in isolation to maximise its own gain, or whether they can be achieved in harmony on the basis of a global consensus for the mutual benefit of all nations.

# Appendix 1

# 'Joint Guarantees' and the Evolution of a World Development Fund: a Scheme

### Guarantee Arrangements

1. It was suggested in Chapter 3 that central bank cooperation which would have the effect of recycling OPEC surpluses off-market and through the IMF, could also facilitate the negotiation of 'jointly shared guarantees' between governments, which alone could place this lending on a longer-term footing. These guarantees in turn could lead to the establishment of a World Development Fund. It is therefore necessary to consider in more detail the alternative guarantee arrangements which might be available for supporting long-term lending.

2. At least three types of guarantee arrangement are open to governments to establish among themselves for the purpose of underwriting any flotations of bonds raised in the capital markets, irrespective of whether they are to underpin any permanent new development agency.

3. The first and simplest type of guarantee would be a 'full joint and several guarantee' of the bonds of the participating governments. Each government would, under such a guarantee, be liable for the full amount of the guaranteed obligations and a bondholder could make a claim against any single guarantor for the full amount due. The guarantor governments could, by arrangement, determine the proportion of their respective liabilities as among themselves, and any guarantor paying a bondholder more than its agreed share could recover from the other guarantors.

4. Secondly, and at the other extreme, would be a 'several guarantee' under

which each government would guarantee only a specified proportion of each bond. This would present greater difficulty for bondholders since, unless special arrangements were made, it would be necessary in the event of a default to make a claim against each guarantor government.

5. A third and intermediate possibility would be an arrangement under which each member government, while giving only a 'several guarantee', would contribute, in an amount based on the proportion of the bonds guaranteed by it, to a fund in which the bondholders would share if there were a default. This approach is illustrated by the Austrian Government Guaranteed Loan (1923-43) arranged by the Financial Committee of the League of Nations. The net effect of such an arrangement would have many of the characteristics of, but would fall short of, a 'full joint and several guarantee'. It is this third approach which may be described as a 'limited joint and several guarantee'.

6. This type of guarantee would be somewhat similar to the arrangement by which the member governments of a development agency 'guarantee' that agency's obligations on the basis of its callable capital. Strictly speaking, bonds issued by the agency are not guaranteed by the agency's member governments. However, in case of a default on its bonds, or to prevent a default, the agency can call for payment of the callable as distinct from paid-in capital of its member governments and use the amounts received to make the required payments on its bonds. Each government's obligation to make payments on such calls is not dependent on payment being made by other member governments and, since successive calls may be made until sufficient funds are available to pay the obligations of the agency, the system is very like a 'joint and several guarantee'. But since each government is liable only to the extent of its uncalled capital, such a system is not equivalent to a 'full joint and several guarantee', as no single government can be liable for the total amount being guaranteed by all participating governments together.

7. It follows from this account of possible guarantee mechanisms that any desired system of guarantees can be established among participating governments prior to the formal setting up of an agency. Indeed, in the case of the Brandt Commission's proposed new institution the transitional stage involving 'jointly shared guarantees' between governments could well take the form of their establishing a system of 'limited joint and several guarantees', along the lines of the Austrian loan guarantee procedure referred to above. This would enable them to raise funds pending the formal establishment of a new institution in a manner which would obviate the need in the first instance for the formal putting in of capital subscriptions. Such a system could also be set up pending the subsequent joining in with the institution of governments which may not initially participate in the guarantees. All that would be

required would be for the guarantor governments to designate an entity endowed with a legal personality – which could indeed be one of the participatory governments – to raise funds on the strength of their collective guarantee. The funds that would be raised could include the proceeds of off-market reserve diversification arrangements referred to earlier, which would have initially been channelled through the IMF, pending the setting up of the selected system of guarantees.

8. Once a system of 'limited joint and several guarantees' has been instituted, the guarantees could be converted subsequently into the callable capital of a permanent lending institution, though further negotiations will be required to determine its paid-in capital. In the light, however, of the difficulties that are likely to arise if negotiations were conducted on a world-wide basis, it has been suggested that both the system of guarantees and the subsequent negotiations for paid-in capital should be conducted sequentially and, to begin with, at the level of interested countries. This will mean that at an early stage 'jointly shared guarantees' among interested governments would have been operative which could lead in the next stage to the setting up of an institution involving these same governments. This approach has been suggested both because of the urgency of the balance of payments needs of non-oil developing countries and because of the existence of a willingess among OPEC governments to proceed somewhat along these lines, as evident by a recent proposal[1] to transform the OPEC Speciál Fund into a Development Agency.

**The OPEC Agency**

9. The two stages suggested above, namely, first the elaboration of a system of 'limited joint and several guarantees' among interested governments and second their conversion into the callable capital of a new institution, could first be applied to the proposal for transforming the OPEC Special Fund into a Development Agency. What would be required, in the first place, is the adoption in the context of the proposal, *mutatis mutandis,* of the mechanism for elaborating 'limited joint and several guarantees' by interested OPEC governments, so that the OPEC Special Fund itself is enabled to disburse monies in advance of the formal commencement of operations of the proposed Agency.

10. The current proposal envisages an Agency with a capital of $20 billion

---

1. Joint proposal by the Algerian and Venezuelan delegations on *The need for additional financial cooperation between OPEC member countries and other developing countries,* presented to the LV Conference of OPEC Ministers, Caracas, 17 December 1979.

to be fully operational by 1983 with half the capital, that is \$10 billion, paid-in. The Agency's operations, however, are expected to commence at the beginning of 1981 on the basis of \$5 billion paid-in capital and a total initial capital of \$10 billion. The difference between paid-in and total capital would constitute callable capital which would support the raising of funds in capital markets on terms yielding normal commercial returns to countries which subscribe to the bonds of the Agency. There is a built-in provision to facilitate the participation of non-OPEC developing countries in the Agency from the outset; the Special Fund's outstanding loans to developing countries, amounting to \$1 billion, will be treated as part of the paid-in capital of the Agency, which would enable loan repayments by developing countries to be counted in their capital subscription.

11. The Agency would undertake the following activities :

(i) financing of balance of payments deficits ;

(ii) financing under favourable terms of economic and social development projects recognised by recipient countries as priority projects, including the development of renewable and non-renewable sources of energy ;

(iii) financing of projects intended to reinforce integration between developing countries in order to promote their collective self-reliance ;

(iv) financing of projects intended to upgrade the value of the raw materials produced by developing countries ;

(v) underwriting of export credits between developing countries, especially in the area of energy supply ;

(vi) financing of commercial operations of developing countries under market conditions ; and

(vii) underwriting loans floated by developing countries on financial markets.

The Agency is thus conceived of as a Third World body designed primarily to promote collective self-reliance within its membership, involving 'jointly shared guarantees' between OPEC and other developing countries.

12. An outstanding feature of the proposal is the conservative capital structure that is envisaged, implying a paid-in capital at all times of 50 per cent. This compares, for instance, with the 20 per cent ratio of the paid-in capital to total capital with which the World Bank commenced operations, and the 7 per cent ratio underlying the World Bank's current capital increase.

The reason for the conservatism is explained in the proposal by the need to utilise part of the Agency's capital to subsidise lending. There are, however, alternative ways of introducing an acceptable element of concessionality while enhancing the lending potential of the $9 billion worth of additional resources which the OPEC members are expected to contribute to the Agency.

13. Assuming that an acceptable degree of concessionality is provided by Third Window terms, a 'once-for-all' contribution of $1 in cash generates the required interest subsidy for $4 worth of lending, provided that the $4 is raised at 8 per cent, roughly the current rate for Deutsche Mark denominated bonds, and that the borrowing is supported by a system of 'joint and several guarantees'. On this basis the undisbursed portion – $2 billion – of the cash amount of $ 2.4 billion with which it is intended to replenish the OPEC Special Fund this year can be treated as a 'once-for-all' interest subsidy contribution for supporting programme lending on Third Window terms. If a similar cash amount for the same purpose were to be available for interest subsidy purposes in 1981, lending up to a total of $16 billion would become possible during 1980-1981. Since $4 billion of the $10 billion contribution called for in the original proposal would have been so set aside, only the balance of $6 billion (of which $1 billion will be the non-OPEC developing country contribution) will remain available to be reckoned, *strictu sensu,* for paid-in capital purposes. This procedure would thus imply the creation of an Agency with a total capitalisation of $22 billion, $6 billion of which will be paid-in capital, with a ratio of paid-in to total capital of 27 per cent; and a 'once-for-all' interest subsidy contribution of $4 billion would enable it to lend up to $16 billion on Third Window terms.

**World Development Fund**

14. Further, if the developed countries were to provide, as suggested in Chapter 3, equal and matching contributions for both interest subsidy and paid-in capital purposes, an embryonic World Development Fund could be established with an initial size of $44 billion. It would have a paid-in capital of $ 12 billion, of which $5 billion would be provided by OPEC countries, another $ 5 billion by developed countries and $ 2 billion by developing countries; the last-mentioned amount would be generated, as under the above proposal for the OPEC Agency, by treating the debt service payments of non-OPEC developing countries as their contribution to the paid-in capital. There would be in addition a 'once-for-all' interest subsidy contribution jointly provided by OPEC and the developed market economies of $8 billion, permitting a total lending on Third Window terms of $32 billion that will have been borrowed in capital markets.

15. With the implementation of the current round of SDR allocations, most of the amount required for the above purposes from developed countries could be raised by drawing on counterpart national currencies in respect of their SDR allocations, thus avoiding any additional burden on their government budgets. A total of SDR 8 billion will be available for the years 1980 and 1981, of which 70 per cent, or nearly SDR 6 billion will accrue to the developed countries under the current rules governing the SDR allocations. The equivalent of over $7 billion, which could voluntarily be parted with in the form of counterpart national currencies, will implement in effect the 'link' proposal now also endorsed by the Brandt Commission without needing an amendment of IMF articles.

16. It would be reasonable to expect that a Fund of this magnitude, involving developed countries as well, would be in a position to widen its range of activities as compared with those listed above for the transformed OPEC Special Fund. Specifically, the missing elements in the current system of development finance as suggested by the Brandt Commission could be added to the functions of the new institution. These would include, in particular, finance for reinforcing regional integration efforts (for providing the necessary external line of credit) and a project focus in the area of energy and food.

17. Finally, it should be noted that, as far as the transitional period is concerned, if the OPEC Special Fund were to proceed on the basis suggested above, the $2 billion cash resources available to it in 1980 would enable it to raise, on the basis of supporting guarantees from OPEC governments, up to $8 billion to be disbursed on Third Window terms by simply using the $2 billion as a 'once-for-all' interest subsidy contribution. This amount of $8 billion would be within the range of additional financing that would be required by non-oil developing countries in 1980 and provide some margin for carrying-over into 1981. A proportion of the funds raised in 1980 could be used to finance a rebate, as suggested in Chapter 3, on the incremental oil-bill of the low-income non-oil developing countries.

18. The bulk of the lending in this transitional phase would need to be for the financing of the balance of payments deficits, which is listed as the first of the functions to be undertaken by the proposed OPEC Agency. This lending would need to be on the basis of conditionality that is, at the same time, stringent enough to encourage the required structural adjustments, for example, to a higher and possibly rising level of prices, and easy enough to encourage countries to have ready recourse to it. While no generalised rule can obviously cover individual cases, this suggests, as a guideline, a degree of conditionality somewhere between the IMF reserve tranche and upper

tranche conditionality, that is, first credit tranche conditionality with modifications. It does not seem useful to specify in any greater detail at this stage the patterns of conditionality within which the Agency should work, except to say that the kinds of modification to current IMF practice recommended in the Brandt Commission's report would apply *a fortiori* to the functions of the Agency from the outset.

# Appendix 2

**Members of the Group of Experts**

| | |
|---|---|
| Prof. H.W. Arndt (Chairman) | Professor of Economics, Research School of Pacific Studies, Australian National University, Canberra. |
| Prof. A.D. Brownlie | Vice-Chancellor, University of Canterbury, New Zealand. |
| Sir Alec Cairncross | Chancellor of the University of Glasgow; formerly Master of St. Peter's College, Oxford and Head of UK Government Economic Service 1964-69. |
| Dr. William G. Demas (Vice-Chairman) | President, Caribbean Development Bank, Barbados. |
| H.E. Dr. Lal Jayawardena | Ambassador of the Republic of Sri Lanka to Belgium, Netherlands and Luxembourg and the European Communities, formerly Secretary to the Treasury and Secretary, Ministry of Finance and Planning, Sri Lanka. |
| H.E. Mr. W.J. Jenkins | Ambassador of Canada to Saudi Arabia; ex-Vice President (Policy), Canadian International Development Agency. |
| Mr. D.C. Mulaisho | Special Assistant (Economic) to the President of Zambia. |
| Mr. Ramon V. Navaratnam | Deputy Secretary-General, Ministry of Finance, Government of Malaysia. |
| Prof. H.M.A. Onitiri | Director, Nigerian Institute of Social and Economic Research, University of Ibadan, Ibadan, Nigeria. |
| Prof. Amartya Sen | Drummond Professor of Political Economy, Oxford University and Fellow of All Souls College, Oxford; formerly Professor of Economics, Delhi School of Economics, India. |

| | |
|---|---|
| **Secretariat** | (Economic Affairs Division, Commonwealth Secretariat) |
| Dr. Bimal Jalan | Director |
| Dr. B. Persaud | Assistant Director |
| Mr. Q.S. Siddiqi | Assistant Director |
| Mr. I.R. Thomas | Chief Economics Officer |